# Scott McFarland

Andrea Kunard

# A Cultivated View
## Scott McFarland
# La réalité aménagée

Canadian Museum of Contemporary Photography
The CMCP is an affiliate of the National Gallery of Canada

Musée canadien de la photographie contemporaine
Le MCPC est affilié au Musée des beaux-arts du Canada

Published in conjunction with the exhibition *Scott McFarland: A Cultivated View*, organized by the Canadian Museum of Contemporary Photography and presented at the National Gallery of Canada, Ottawa, from 11 April to 13 September 2009.

The catalogue has been produced by the Publications Division of the National Gallery of Canada, Ottawa.
Chief of Publications: Serge Thériault
English Editor: Caroline Wetherilt
French Editor: Marie-Nicole Cimon
Picture Editor: Anne Tessier
Production: Anne Tessier
Translation (English to French): Marie-Josée Arcand



Printed by St. Joseph Print Group, Ottawa

Cover: *Fountain Study, Late Fall; Cedrus atlantica, Acer palmatum, Populus nigra*, 2004 (detail, plate 2)



PRINTED IN CANADA

ISBN 978-0-88884-861-1

**Distribution**
ABC Art Books Canada
www.abcartbookscanada.com
info@abcartbookscanada.com

Publié à l'occasion de l'exposition *Scott McFarland . La réalité aménagée*, organisée par le Musée canadien de la photographie contemporaine et présentée au Musée des beaux-arts du Canada, à Ottawa, du 11 avril au 13 septembre 2009.

Le catalogue a été produit par la Division des publications du Musée des beaux-arts du Canada, Ottawa.
Chef des publications : Serge Thériault
Réviseure anglophone : Caroline Wetherilt
Réviseure francophone : Marie-Nicole Cimon
Iconographe : Anne Tessier
Responsable de la production : Anne Tessier
Traductrice (de l'anglais au français) : Marie-Josée Arcand



Imprimé par St.Joseph Print Group, Ottawa

Couverture : *Étude d'une fontaine, à la fin de l'automne. Cedrus atlantica, Acer palmatum, Populus nigra*, 2004 (détail, planche 2)



IMPRIMÉ AU CANADA

ISBN 978-0-88884-861-1

**Distribution**
ABC Livres d'art Canada
www.abcartbookscanada.com
info@abcartbookscanada.com

## Contents



## Sommaire

## Foreword

It is with great pleasure that the Canadian Museum of Contemporary Photography presents *Scott McFarland: A Cultivated View*. Since graduating from the University of British Columbia just over ten years ago, Scott McFarland has become distinguished for his beautifully crafted photographs. He has exhibited in major art institutions, both national and international, such as the Victoria and Albert Museum, London; The Museum of Modern Art, New York; the Vancouver Art Gallery; and The Montreal Museum of Fine Arts. Within his overall oeuvre, projects have concentrated on subjects ranging from traditional commercial darkrooms to a coastal cabin nestled in the rainforest of British Columbia's Sunshine Coast. A major component of this exhibition focuses on his projects that depict a refined engagement with the natural world. Gardens are one predominant theme; human interaction with animals is another. The world the artist reveals for us is both real and fictive. Initial views are taken with a large format camera. Negatives are then scanned and combined to create a seamless view. Through the selective framing of the camera and the digital weaving of images, the artist creates a thoughtful and exquisitely detailed, self-contained world, one that provides the spectator with a rich viewing experience.



We are grateful to Scott McFarland for his involvement in the preparation of the exhibition and catalogue. We also thank curator Andrea Kunard for leading the exhibition to fruition and for her insightful catalogue text. We are also indebted to Project Manager Julie Hodgson, Chief of Exhibitions Christine Sadler, and Chief of Publications Serge Thériault. In addition, we wish to thank Monte Clark and Daniel Faria and staff at the Monte Clark galleries in Vancouver and Toronto, as well as Jennifer Loh at Regen Projects in Los Angeles.

Finally, we are indebted to the Albert and Temmy Latner Family Foundation for the generous support of the catalogue and to the Families of Steven Latner and Michael Latner, in particular, for lending to the exhibition. We also extend grateful thanks to Aaron Latner and other lenders: Byron Aceman; David Allison and Chris Nicholson; Steven Casey; Daniel Faria; Matt Hammatt; William J. Hokin Collection; Mike MacBain; Michael Nininger; Enrico Pallotta and Brigitte Laforest; Karen and Richard Pilosof; Susan and Michael Rich; Steve F. Roth; William and Ruth True; Christopher Wood; RBC Royal Bank; Monte Clark Gallery, Vancouver and Toronto; Union Gallery, London, UK; Private Collections; and Scott McFarland.

Martha Hanna
Director, Canadian Museum of Contemporary Photography

Marc Mayer
Director, National Gallery of Canada

## Avant-propos

C'est avec un grand plaisir que le Musée canadien de la photographie contemporaine présente *Scott McFarland. La réalité aménagée*. Depuis l'obtention de son diplôme de l'University of British Columbia il y a à peine plus de dix ans, Scott McFarland s'est forgé une solide renommée pour ses photographies superbement construites. Il a exposé dans de grandes institutions artistiques, tant nationales qu'internationales, dont le Victoria and Albert Museum, à Londres, le Museum of Modern Art, à New York, le Musée des beaux-arts de Vancouver et le Musée des beaux-arts de Montréal. Son œuvre aborde des thèmes aussi variés que les laboratoires de développement photo commerciaux traditionnels et un chalet en bord de mer niché dans la forêt pluviale de la Sunshine Coast en Colombie-Britannique. Cette exposition met notamment l'accent sur des projets qui portent un regard ciselé sur la nature : les jardins et l'interaction de l'humain avec les animaux. Le monde que l'artiste nous révèle est à la fois réel et fictif. Il se sert d'un appareil photo grand format, il scanne ensuite les négatifs, qu'il combine pour créer une image cohérente. Grâce au cadrage sélectif de l'appareil photographique et au tissage numérique, l'artiste crée un univers autonome, réfléchi et délicieusement détaillé, qui fait vivre au spectateur une riche expérience visuelle.

Nous tenons à remercier Scott McFarland pour sa participation à la préparation de l'exposition et du catalogue. Nous remercions également la conservatrice Andrea Kunard pour avoir mené à bien le projet d'exposition et pour la pertinence du texte qu'elle a écrit en vue du catalogue. Nous sommes aussi redevables à Julie Hodgson, gestionnaire de projet, Christine Sadler, chef, Gestion des expositions, et Serge Thériault, chef des Publications. Nous désirons en outre exprimer notre gratitude à Monte Clark, Daniel Faria et au personnel des galeries Monte Clark, de même qu'à Jennifer Loh de Regen Projects.

Enfin, nous sommes reconnaissants à l'Albert and Temmy Latner Family Foundation pour son soutien généreux au catalogue et aux familles de Steven Latner et de Michael Latner, en particulier, pour leur prêt à l'exposition. Nous remercions également sincèrement Aaron Latner et les autres prêteurs : Byron Aceman, David Allison et Chris Nicholson, Steven Casey, Daniel Faria, Matt Hammatt, la collection William J. Hokin, Mike MacBain, Michael Nininger, Enrico Pallotta et Brigitte Laforest, Karen et Richard Pilosof, Susan et Michael Rich, Steve F. Roth, William et Ruth True, Christopher Wood, la RBC Banque Royale, la Monte Clark Gallery de Vancouver et Toronto, l'Union Gallery de Londres, au R.-U., des collections privées, ainsi que Scott McFarland.

Martha Hanna
Directrice, Musée canadien de la photographie contemporaine

Marc Mayer
Directeur, Musée des beaux-arts du Canada

## Message from the Sponsor

The Albert and Temmy Latner Family Foundation is extremely honoured to lend its support to the exhibition catalogue for *Scott McFarland: A Cultivated View* at the National Gallery of Canada.

In the busy world of contemporary photography, Scott McFarland has distinguished himself among a myriad of picture-takers who have emerged throughout his generation. As spectators, we are subtly confronted with his careful construction of sculptural images – images that capture a sublime dimension of space and time.

The Latner Family proudly continues to collect the works of Scott McFarland. We applaud the Canadian Museum of Contemporary Photography and the National Gallery of Canada for hosting this exhibition of this important young Canadian artist's work.

## Mot du commanditaire



L'Albert and Temmy Latner Family Foundation est très fière d'accorder son soutien au catalogue accompagnant l'exposition *Scott McFarland. La réalité aménagée*, tenue au Musée des beaux-arts du Canada.

Dans le monde effervescent de la photographie contemporaine, Scott McFarland se distingue parmi une myriade de chasseurs d'images de sa génération. Comme spectateurs, nous sommes subtilement mis en présence de sa construction méticuleuse d'images sculpturales – des images qui saisissent une dimension sublime de l'espace et du temps.

La famille Latner se fait un honneur de continuer à enrichir sa collection des œuvres de Scott McFarland. Nous remercions chaleureusement le Musée canadien de la photographie contemporaine ainsi que le Musée des beaux-arts du Canada de présenter cette exposition du travail de cet important jeune artiste canadien.

Andrea Kunard

# A Cultivated View

# La réalité aménagée

Over the last decade, Scott McFarland has produced bodies of work that engage with different aspects of photography. The *Laboratory* series (2002 continuing) depicts photographic processes, while *Cabin* (2001–04) and *Berlin* (2004 continuing) are studies on place and explore the interrelation of art and document. This exhibition examines these concerns within another dominant theme in McFarland's work – human relations with the natural world, as seen in his series *Gardens* (2001–06), *Hampstead* (2005 continuing) and *Empire* (2003 continuing). Focusing on gardens, landscape views and animals found in particular sites such as zoos, farms and stables, McFarland's approach is both descriptive and metaphoric. In addition to carefully crafting his scene to describe the garden's physical state, McFarland's choice and handling of subject matter incorporate elements that reference photographic processes and the history of art and photography. The images, rich in cultural significance, express the complementary workings of conceptual and aesthetic factors all the while holding various characteristics of art and photography in ambiguous relation.



## Gardens and Cultivated Nature

A site of utopian impulse, the garden represents a shaping of nature to human purpose, a sense of regulation, order and control. For some, it evokes a Biblical scene of pastoral bliss, harmony of spirit and mind, and happy cohabitation with flora and fauna. The drudgery of garden creation – being mired in mud, weeding and pruning – is rarely depicted. In photographs of stately gardens, the very machine that produces them is also often missing. The view is always outward and descriptive, the operator/photographer/artist (the names intermingle) carefully avoiding any transcription of his or her presence in the final image. The garden, exorcised of labour, is envisioned as a luxuriant, fruitful and self-sustaining place, a site of leisure, inspiration and philosophical musings where mind and matter merge to a "green thought in a green shade."[1]

In his *Gardens* series, which concentrates on private gardens found in Vancouver's affluent West Side, McFarland unites the desired view of the garden with collaboratively staged scenes of maintenance. Hired workers spray plants, inspect leaves, trap animals and filter ponds. In some cases, the exacting composition and pose of workers underscore the idea of human activity blending with nature, as seen in

Tout au long de la dernière décennie, Scott McFarland a produit des corpus d'œuvres qui traitent de différents aspects de la photographie. La série *Laboratoire* (à partir de 2002) illustre les procédés photographiques, alors que *Chalet* (2001–2004) et *Berlin* (à partir de 2004) sont des études de lieux, qui explorent l'interrelation entre art et documentation. La présente exposition se penche sur ces centres d'intérêt au travers d'un autre thème dominant dans l'œuvre de McFarland : les relations qu'entretient l'humain avec le monde naturel, abordées dans les séries *Jardins* (2001–2006), *Hampstead* (à partir de 2005) et *Empire* (à partir de 2003). Centrée sur les jardins, les paysages et les animaux que l'on trouve dans des endroits particuliers comme les zoos, les fermes et les écuries, l'approche de McFarland est à la fois descriptive et métaphorique. Outre le soin qu'il apporte dans la composition de sa scène pour décrire le jardin dans son état physique, McFarland, dans son choix et son traitement du sujet, intègre également des éléments faisant référence aux procédés photographiques et à l'histoire de l'art et de la photographie. Les images, riches en signifiants culturels, expriment les mécanismes complémentaires de facteurs conceptuels et esthétiques tout en véhiculant, dans une relation ambiguë, diverses caractéristiques de l'art et de la photographie.



## Les jardins et la nature aménagée

Lieu de pulsions utopiques, le jardin incarne le façonnage de la nature selon les *desiderata* de l'humain, un sens de la régulation, de l'ordre et du contrôle. Pour certains, il évoque une scène biblique de félicité bucolique, d'harmonie de l'esprit et de la pensée, et d'une cohabitation heureuse entre flore et faune. Le labeur que suppose la création d'un jardin – les pieds dans la boue, le désherbage et la taille – est rarement illustré. Dans les photographies de jardins imposants, la machinerie qui sert à la réalisation de ces derniers est également souvent évacuée. La vue est toujours extérieure et descriptive, l'opérateur/photographe/artiste (les noms se mélangent) évitant soigneusement toute allusion à sa propre présence dans l'image finale. Le jardin, exorcisé du travail, est vu comme un lieu luxuriant, fécond et autosuffisant, un site de loisirs, d'inspiration et de méditations philosophiques où esprit et matière se rejoignent en une « pensée verte dans une ombre verte »[1].

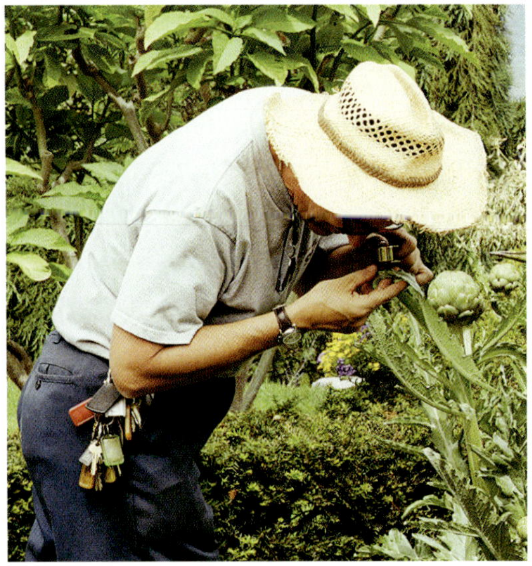

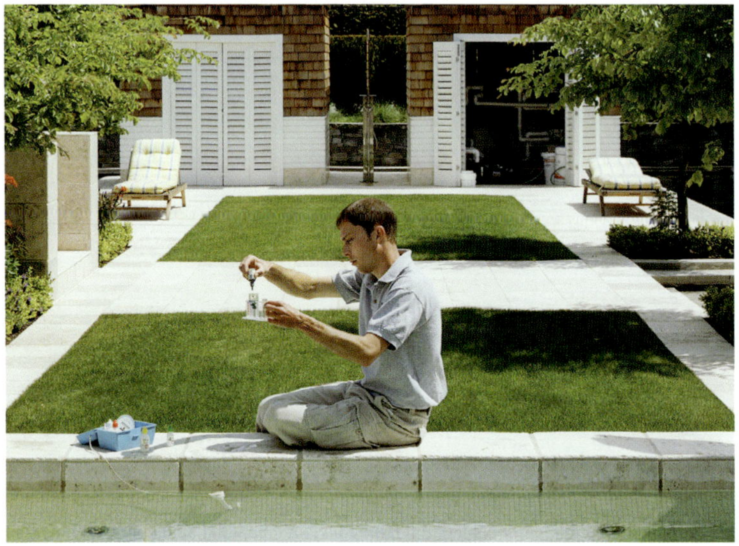



*Inspecting, Allan O'Connor Searches for Botrytis cinerea* (fig. 1, plate 5), where the arched backs of the gardeners echo the curved bends of the hedges and shrubbery in which they work.

For McFarland, gardening and landscaping activities are integrally linked to photographic processes as the two share many common elements. Both make use of chemicals that require constant monitoring and careful measurement: photography with developer fluids, stop baths and fixatives, and gardening and landscaping with fertilizers, pesticides and other additives (see fig. 2). For example, in *Pouring, Ben Kubomiwa Treating Fountain with Potassium Permanganate* (plate 1), the brilliant magenta solution the gardener pours into the pond to establish pH balance recalls the colour of an exhausted stop bath in photographic development. The connection between gardening and photography can also be seen in *Inspecting, Allan O'Connor Searches for Botrytis cinerea*, where Allan O'Connor's use of a magnifying device to inspect leaves suggests the application of a loop on the camera's ground glass to ensure sharp focus and high detail (fig. 1).

**Fig. 1** Scott McFarland, *Inspecting, Allan O'Connor Searches for Botrytis cinerea*, 2003. From the series *Gardens* (detail)

**Fig. 2** Scott McFarland, *Analyzing, Ryan Otto Conducts Water Test*, 2003. From the series *Gardens* (detail)

Dans sa série *Jardins*, qui se concentre sur les jardins privés que l'on trouve dans le quartier cossu de West Side à Vancouver, McFarland réunit la vue rêvée du jardin et des mises en scène qui illustrent l'entretien des lieux. Des ouvriers engagés à cette fin pulvérisent les plantes, inspectent les feuilles, piègent les animaux et filtrent les bassins. Dans certains cas, la composition et la pose étudiée des ouvriers soulignent l'idée de l'activité humaine se fondant avec la nature, comme on peut le voir dans *Inspecter, Allan O'Connor cherche du Botrytis cinerea* (fig. 1, planche 5), où le dos arqué des jardiniers fait écho aux courbes des haies et massifs sur lesquels ils travaillent.

Pour McFarland, les activités de jardinage et d'aménagement paysager sont intégralement liées aux procédés photographiques, les deux ayant de nombreux éléments en commun – dont le recours à des produits chimiques exigeant une surveillance constante et des dosages minutieux : la photographie avec les révélateurs, les bains d'arrêt et les fixateurs, le jardinage avec les engrais, les pesticides et d'autres adjuvants (voir fig. 2). Ainsi, dans *Verser, Ben Kubomiwa traite la fontaine avec du permanganate de potassium* (planche 1), la solution magenta brillante que le jardinier verse dans le bassin pour vérifier l'équilibre du pH rappelle la couleur d'un bain d'arrêt épuisé en développement photographique. Le lien entre jardinage et photographie est également apparent dans *Inspecter, Allan O'Connor cherche du Botrytis cinerea*, où l'utilisation par Allan O'Connor d'un appareil grossissant pour inspecter les feuilles suggère l'ajout d'une lentille macro sur le verre de visée de l'appareil photo pour s'assurer d'une mise au point nette et d'un haut niveau de détail (fig. 1).

La connexion entre jardinage et photographie remonte aux origines mêmes de la technique photographique. William Henry Fox Talbot (1800–1877), créateur du procédé négatif-positif qui deviendra la base de la photographie moderne, est un jardinier amateur passionné. Il va développer son procédé photographique afin d'améliorer la méthode alors en vigueur pour décrire les plantes (voir fig. 3). Talbot mène ses activités horticoles – la construction de serres et la représentation minutieuse des plantes – en parallèle à ses recherches sur les produits chimiques, les papiers et les lentilles[2].

**Fig. 1** Scott McFarland, *Inspecter, Allan O'Connor cherche du Botrytis cinerea*, 2003. De la série *Jardins* (détail)

**Fig. 2** Scott McFarland, *Analyser, Ryan Otto teste l'eau*, 2003. De la série *Jardins* (détail)

The link between gardening and photography goes back to the very origins of the photographic medium. William Henry Fox Talbot (1800–1877), creator of the negative-positive process that became the basis of modern photography, was an enthusiastic amateur gardener. He developed his photographic process as an improvement on the day's method of recording plants (see fig. 3). Talbot's horticultural activities – the construction of greenhouses and careful delineation of plants – took place alongside his research into chemicals, papers and lenses.[2]

McFarland's photographs also challenge categories of art and document. In terms of the latter, the photograph in its descriptive capacity carries the weight of authority and order, grounded in a cultural belief in the objectivity of the medium. On one level, the detailed precision and startling clarity of McFarland's photographs present the world as something intensely observed and scrutinized. In some cases, as especially occurs in views of the Huntington Botanical Garden in San Marino, California, taxonomic captions such as *echinocactus grusonii* further support a documentary approach with their connection to scientific classificatory schemes that neatly arrange reality.



This idea of the document, however, is challenged by the artistry of the imagery. McFarland uses film and a large format camera to take his shots. He then scans his negatives and digitally combines them to present a singular seamless photograph. This capacity to transform the world is echoed in his very subject matter. Gardens are frequently unnatural places. They are often comprised of various species of non-indigenous plants included for aesthetic effect. In some images, McFarland also indicates an entropic element within this activity of control; at its edges, the garden begins to break down. Yet, as the garden is viewed more as a composed site, so the photographer works to create a controlled vision of its depiction, an expectation of nature photographers since the nineteenth century. However, in the twenty-first century, digital manipulation allows the photographer to act as the master painter.

**Fig. 3** William Henry Fox Talbot, *Leaf of a Plant*, before 14 February 1844, salted paper print. National Gallery of Canada, Ottawa (33487.20)

One artist who figures strongly here is John Constable (1776–1837), the *plein air*, proto-Impressionist painter who delighted in capturing the ephemeral qualities of light and sky. One of Constable's richest periods of studying skies, an activity he termed "skying,"[3] occurred on Hampstead Heath in London.[4] McFarland has travelled to this area on several occasions, and the atmospheric conditions that enthralled Constable

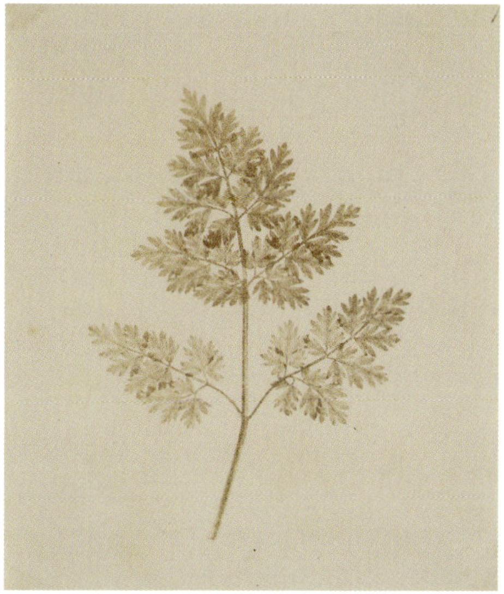

**Fig. 3** William Henry Fox Talbot, *Feuille d'une plante*, avant 14 février 1844, épreuve sur papier salé. Musée des beaux-arts du Canada, Ottawa (33487.20)



Les photographies de McFarland remettent aussi en question la catégorisation entre art et documentation. Pour ce qui est de cette dernière, la photographie dans sa capacité descriptive représente l'autorité et l'ordre, ancrée qu'elle est dans une foi culturelle en l'objectivité du médium. À un certain niveau, les œuvres de McFarland, à la précision toute en détail et à la netteté saisissante, présentent le monde comme quelque chose d'intensément observé et scruté. Dans certains cas, comme cela transparaît particulièrement dans les vues du Huntington Botanical Garden à San Marino, en Californie, les légendes taxinomiques telles que *echinocactus grusonii* viennent renforcer une approche documentaire par leurs liens avec les systèmes de classification scientifique qui organisent avec soin la réalité.

L'idée de documentation, toutefois, est remise en question par la dimension artistique de l'imagerie. McFarland utilise la pellicule et un appareil photographique grand format pour prendre ses clichés. Il scanne ensuite ses négatifs et les combine numériquement pour présenter une photographie étonnamment cohérente. Cette

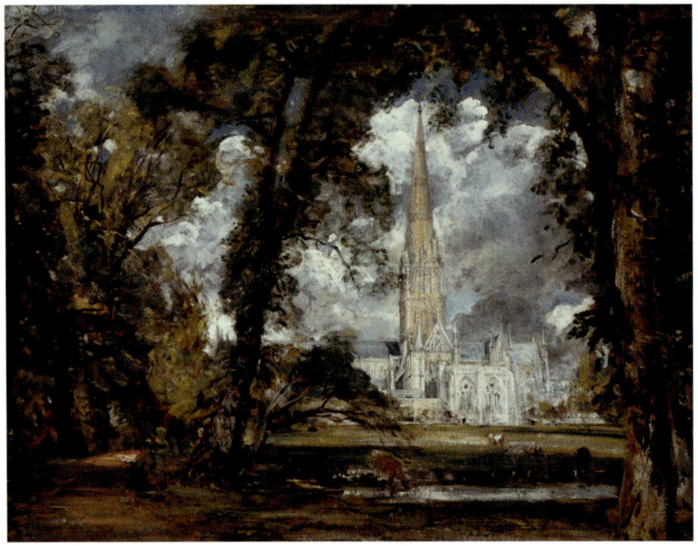

Fig. 4 John Constable, *Salisbury Cathedral from the Bishop's Grounds,* 1820, oil on canvas. National Gallery of Canada, Ottawa (18687)

from the heights of the Heath also preoccupy McFarland – the transitory nature of light and cloud a challenge to photography's inherent character to resolutely fix its subject matter. McFarland skirts this problem somewhat through a continued study of skies presented in an idiosyncratic use of "editions." An edition is usually understood as a limited number of identical reproductions produced for sale. McFarland utilizes this idea of restricting copies to investigate effects of sky, an idea he derived from Constable's painting *Salisbury Cathedral from the Bishop's Grounds* (fig. 4), which exists in six versions, each with a different sky. In McFarland's *Hampstead* works, the site remains fixed, but the skies differ. Through this re-presentation of place, the artist calls attention to how the effects of light and cloud patterns affect the mood and feel of a landscape.

As much as the *Hampstead* series is indebted to Constable's painterly sensibility, photographically it and other sky studies also allude to the work of the nineteenth-century French photographer Gustave Le Gray (1820–1884) and his combination printing methods. In the nineteenth century, if photographers timed their photographic plates to capacité à transformer le monde trouve écho dans son sujet même. Les jardins sont en général des lieux artificiels. Ils abritent souvent diverses espèces de plantes non indigènes que l'on a choisies pour leur effet esthétique. Dans certaines images, McFarland montre également un élément entropique au sein même de cette activité de contrôle; à sa lisière, le jardin commence à se défaire. Pourtant, le jardin est plutôt vu comme un lieu organisé, et le photographe travaille donc à créer une image contrôlée de ce qu'il illustre, une aspiration des photographes de la nature qui remonte au XIXe siècle. Cependant, au XXIe siècle, la manipulation numérique permet au photographe d'agir tel un grand peintre.

L'artiste John Constable (1776–1837), peintre de plein air et proto-impressionniste captivé par le rendu des propriétés éphémères de la lumière et du ciel, est très présent ici. Une des périodes les plus fastes pour Constable dans l'étude des ciels, une activité qu'il nomme *skying*[3], est celle où il fréquente Hampstead Heath à Londres[4]. McFarland va s'y rendre à plusieurs reprises, et les conditions atmosphériques qui avaient fasciné Constable depuis les hauteurs du Heath touchent également McFarland, la nature fugace de la lumière et des nuages représentant un défi pour la pose résolue du sujet, une caractéristique inhérente à la photographie. McFarland esquive quelque peu ce problème par une étude en continu des ciels présentée dans une utilisation idiosyncrasique de « tirages ». Par tirage, on entend habituellement un nombre limité de reproductions identiques, produites pour la vente. McFarland se sert de cette idée de copies en quantité restreinte pour explorer les effets du ciel, idée trouvant son origine dans le tableau de Constable, *La cathédrale de Salisbury vue des jardins de l'évêché* (fig. 4), qui existe en six versions, chacune avec un ciel différent. Dans les œuvres de la série *Hampstead* de McFarland, le site reste inchangé, mais les ciels diffèrent. Au travers de cette re-présentation du lieu, l'artiste attire l'attention sur la manière dont les effets de la lumière et des motifs formés par les nuages influencent l'ambiance et l'atmosphère qui se dégagent du paysage.

**Fig. 4** John Constable, *La cathédrale de Salisbury vue des jardins de l'évêché*, 1820, huile sur toile. Musée des beaux-arts du Canada, Ottawa (18687)

Si la série *Hampstead* doit beaucoup à la sensibilité picturale de Constable, sur un plan photographique elle fait allusion, ainsi que d'autres études de ciel, au travail du photographe français du XIXe siècle Gustave Le Gray (1820–1884) et à ses

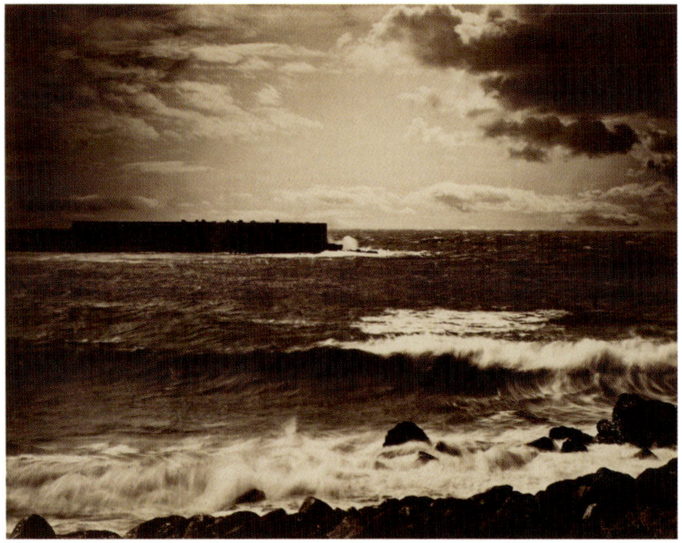



Fig. 5 Gustave Le Gray, *Wave – Sète*, 1857, albumen silver print. National Gallery of Canada, Ottawa (31460)

depict detail in a dark area of the shot, the sky would be overexposed, scorched to a desolate blankness. Cloud scenes were taken separately and then combined onto a scene, a technique honed to an art in the case of Le Gray, but also practiced by many commercial photographers who kept a cache of sky negatives in their possession. Le Gray's photographs, part of a nineteenth-century movement to recognize photography as art, were considered to be expressive of deep emotions, less "taken" than created (see fig. 5).

### Animals and Artistry

Through his careful crafting of photographs, McFarland presents a genteel vision of nature and the place of humans within it. Animals, usually domesticated ones, stand quietly by their human keepers; a steady hand on its face calms a horse being shod, and dogs stand alert beside their masters. The extended view format presents subject matter as a stately tableau; a gentle zookeeper feeds placid, lumbering porcupines in a stylized natural setting; young women groom docile horses in a bucolic orchard filled méthodes de tirage combiné. Au XIXe siècle, lorsque les photographes règlent leurs plaques photographiques pour dépeindre un détail dans une zone sombre de l'image, le ciel se retrouve surexposé, brûlé en un vide désolé. Les scènes de ciel sont prises séparément, puis combinées à une scène existante, une technique élevée au rang d'art dans le cas de Le Gray, mais également pratiquée par de nombreux photographes commerciaux, qui conservent une panoplie de négatifs de ciel à portée de main. Les œuvres de Le Gray, qui fait partie au XIXe siècle d'un mouvement visant à faire reconnaître la photographie en tant qu'art, sont alors considérées comme exprimant des émotions profondes, et moins « prises » que créées (voir fig. 5).

### Les animaux et l'art

Dans ses photographies soigneusement mises en scène, McFarland présente une vision raffinée de la nature et de la place des humains en son sein. Les animaux, en général domestiques, se tiennent sagement près de leurs gardiens; une main ferme sur sa tête calme un cheval que l'on vient de ferrer, et des chiens restent vigilants au côté de leurs maîtres. Avec le format en vue élargie, le sujet est traité à la manière d'un tableau empreint de majesté : un gardien de zoo nourrit avec douceur des porcs-épics placides et lourds, dans un décor naturel stylisé; de jeunes femmes toilettent des chevaux dociles dans un verger bucolique rempli de pousses printanières; des gens sont dans un bois, et leurs chiens, fidèles compagnons, sont pourtant distraits par la compagnie les uns des autres. Les univers humain et animal sont dépeints comme étant intimement entrelacés, une vision que complète la méthode de McFarland consistant à créer une imagerie qui emprunte aux propriétés tant numériques qu'analogiques de la photographie.

**Fig. 5** Gustave Le Gray, *Grande vague – Sète*, 1857, épreuve à l'albumine argentique. Musée des beaux-arts du Canada, Ottawa (31460)

Par cette manière hybride de travailler, l'artiste montre notre relation avec la nature comme une interaction subtile entre fait et fiction. Cette idée est exprimée de manière concise dans *Cheval en marche arrière, Victoria Moes s'entraîne avec Oscar* (fig. 6), qui représente une jeune fille engagée dans une manœuvre équestre. McFarland compose l'œuvre numériquement pour placer les pattes du cheval dans une relation improbable. La photographie fait référence au débat historique

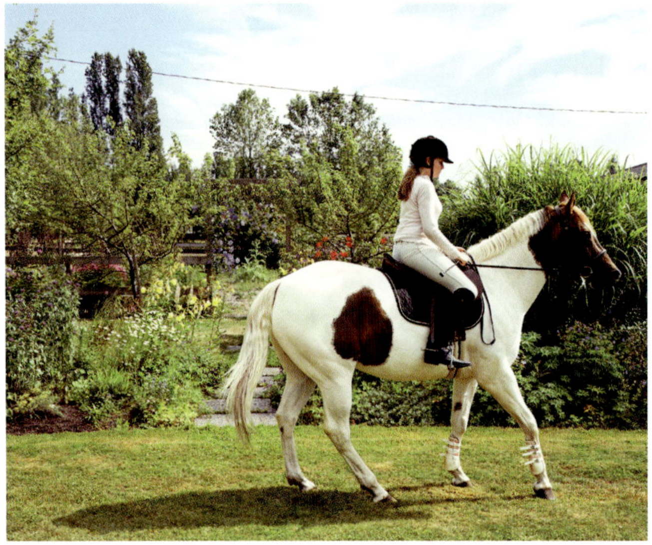



with spring growth; people appear in a wood, their dogs, although faithful companions, nonetheless distracted by one another's company. Animal and human worlds are depicted as intimately intertwined, a vision complemented by McFarland's method of creating imagery that exploits both digital and analogue photographic properties.

Through this hybrid manner of working, the artist demonstrates our relation with nature as a subtle interplay of fact and fiction. This idea is succinctly expressed in *Reverse Horse, Victoria Moes Practices with Oscar* (fig. 6), which depicts a girl engaged in an equestrian maneuver. McFarland has digitally composed the work to place the legs of the horse in false relation. The photograph references the historic debate regarding the position of the horse's legs at full gallop, solved by Eadweard Muybridge (1830–1904) in 1877 through a series of trip wires linked to cameras that broke the gallop into successive images (see fig. 7). Artists who had formerly struggled to render such action now had irrefutable visual reference material to work with. Our era, less impressed with such positivist projects, has the means to digitally "reverse" this discovery and, by

**Fig. 6** Scott McFarland, *Reverse Horse, Victoria Moes Practices with Oscar*, 2008

**Fig. 7** Eadweard Muybridge, *"Annie G." galloping*, c. June 1884–11 May 1886, printed November 1887, collotype. Gift of Dr. Robert W. Crook, Ottawa, 1981. National Gallery of Canada, Ottawa (31880)

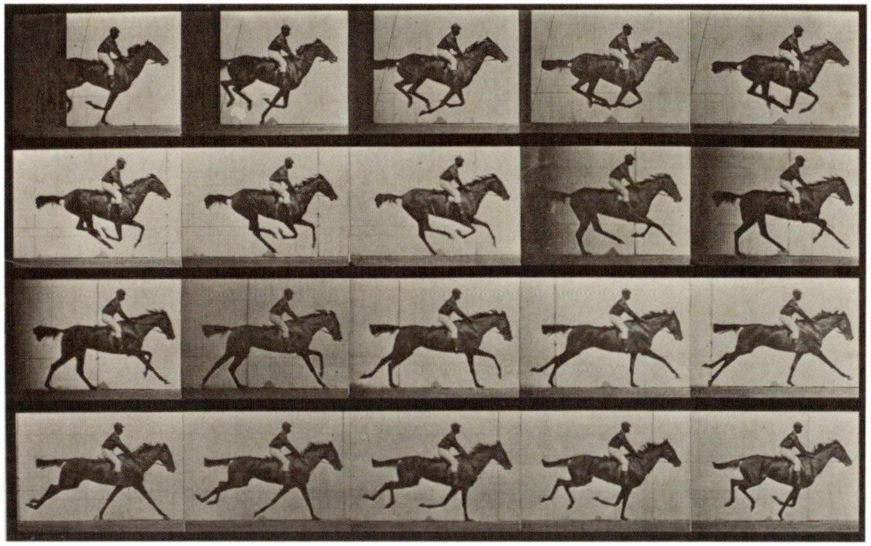



**Fig. 6** Scott McFarland, *Cheval en marche arrière, Victoria Moes s'entraîne avec Oscar*, 2008

**Fig. 7** Eadweard Muybridge, « *Annie G.* » *au galop*, v. juin 1884 – 11 mai 1886, tiré en novembre 1887, phototype. Don du Dr Robert W. Crook, Ottawa, 1981. Musée des beaux-arts du Canada, Ottawa (31880)

concernant la position des pattes du cheval en plein galop, une question résolue par Eadweard Muybridge (1830–1904) en 1877 grâce à une série de fils de déclenchement reliés à des appareils photo qui découpent le galop en images successives (voir fig. 7). Les artistes qui se sont efforcés par le passé de rendre une telle action ont dès lors un matériel visuel irréfutable avec lequel travailler. Notre époque, moins impressionnée par de tels projets positivistes, offre les moyens d'« inverser » numériquement cette découverte et, ce faisant, place le statut de « preuve » photographique en tandem avec le talent artistique et la créativité liés à la production photographique.

*Cheval en marche arrière* offre une illustration doublement artificielle de la nature; la manipulation numérique du pas souligne l'anormalité de la manœuvre équestre de recul. La recomposition de la nature, pour qu'elle se conforme aux besoins des humains, est également apparente dans *Enclos des porcs-épics (Hystrix africae australis), Zoologischer Garten, Berlin* (planche 32), où des porcs-épics se so doing, place the status of photographic "proof" in tandem with the artistry and creativity of photographic production.

*Reverse Horse* renders nature doubly artificial; the digital alteration of the gait emphasizes the unnatural quality of the equestrian back-up maneuver. The reconstruction of nature to suit human purpose is also seen in *Display for Porcupines (Hystrix africae australis), Zoologischer Garten, Berlin* (plate 32), where porcupines trundle about in a zoo pit, sniffing carrots and apples, the reconstruction of their natural habitat at obvious odds with the presence of high-rise buildings in the background. The zoo pit acts as a frame in which to gaze at an idea of nature, as seen in the faces of the contented family in the photo who smile benevolently at the spiny creatures.

McFarland's photographs, like the reconstructions of nature in zoos and gardens, retain this idea of an unimpeded relation with nature. His very use of analogue film to gather raw working material also recalls the belief that the photograph maintains an unhindered relation with the real. In his book *Camera Lucida* (1980), the French cultural critic Roland Barthes (1915–1980) mused that because light rays emanating from a subject produce chemical reactions on a negative, the photograph contains a direct trace of the person that continues even after their death. Grieving the death of his mother, Barthes fixed on a photograph, never reproduced for the reader, taken of her as a child in a setting called "The Winter Garden." This promise of the garden, that it maintains a place of timelessness and innocence, is also held in McFarland's works. However, the further application of technologies to the image disperses Barthes' coveted connection to the past into code. Fragmented, recombined and staged, the images maintain a constructed and artificial character. There is an allusion to what has been, but the certainty of its truthfulness, even if only partly believed in or desired, is set into constant and irresolute play.



**Notes**

1 Andrew Marvell, "The Garden", 17th-century poem.

2 Katie Fretwell, "Fox Talbot's Botanic Garden," *Apollo Magazine*, vol. CLIX, no. 506 (April 2004), pp. 25–28.

3 John E. Thorne, *John Constable's Skies: A Fusion of Art and Science* (London: Continuum International Publishing Group, 1999), p. 55.

4 *Ibid*, p. 22.

meuvent lourdement dans une fosse de zoo, en reniflant carottes et pommes, la recomposition de leur habitat naturel étant en contradiction flagrante avec la présence de grands immeubles à l'arrière-plan. La fosse joue le rôle d'un cadre dans lequel on contemplerait une idée de la nature, tel que l'illustrent les visages de la famille satisfaite que l'on voit dans la photo, qui sourient avec bienveillance aux créatures spinifères.

Les photographies de McFarland, tout comme les recompositions de la nature dans les zoos et les jardins, véhiculent cette idée d'une relation sans entraves avec celle-ci. Son utilisation même de films analogiques pour réunir un matériau brut rappelle également cette conviction que le photographe maintient une relation libre avec le réel. Dans son livre *La chambre claire* (1980), le critique culturel français Roland Barthes (1915–1980) réfléchit au fait que, parce que les rayons lumineux émanant d'un sujet produisent des réactions chimiques sur le négatif, la photographie contient une trace directe de la personne, qui perdure même après sa mort. Affecté par le décès de sa mère, Barthes s'arrête sur une photographie d'elle, jamais reproduite pour le lecteur, qui la montre enfant dans un décor appelé « Le Jardin d'Hiver ». Cette promesse du jardin, selon laquelle celui-ci est dépositaire de l'intemporalité et de l'innocence, est également présente dans les œuvres de McFarland. Toutefois, le recours plus poussé aux technologies dans l'image décompose le lien désiré de Barthes vers le passé en un code. Fragmentées, recomposées et mises en scène, les images conservent un caractère construit et artificiel. On y trouve une allusion à ce qui a été, mais la certitude de leur véracité, même si elle n'est crue ou désirée qu'en partie, s'installe dans un jeu à la fois constant et hésitant.



**Notes**

**1** Andrew Marvell, « The Garden », poème du XVIIe siècle.

**2** Katie Fretwell, « Fox Talbot's Botanic Garden », *Apollo Magazine*, vol. CLIX, n° 506 (avril 2004), p. 25-28.

**3** John E. Thorne, *John Constable's Skies: A Fusion of Art and Science*, Londres, Continuum International Publishing Group, 1999, p. 55.

**4** *Ibid*, p. 22.

# Plates

# Planches

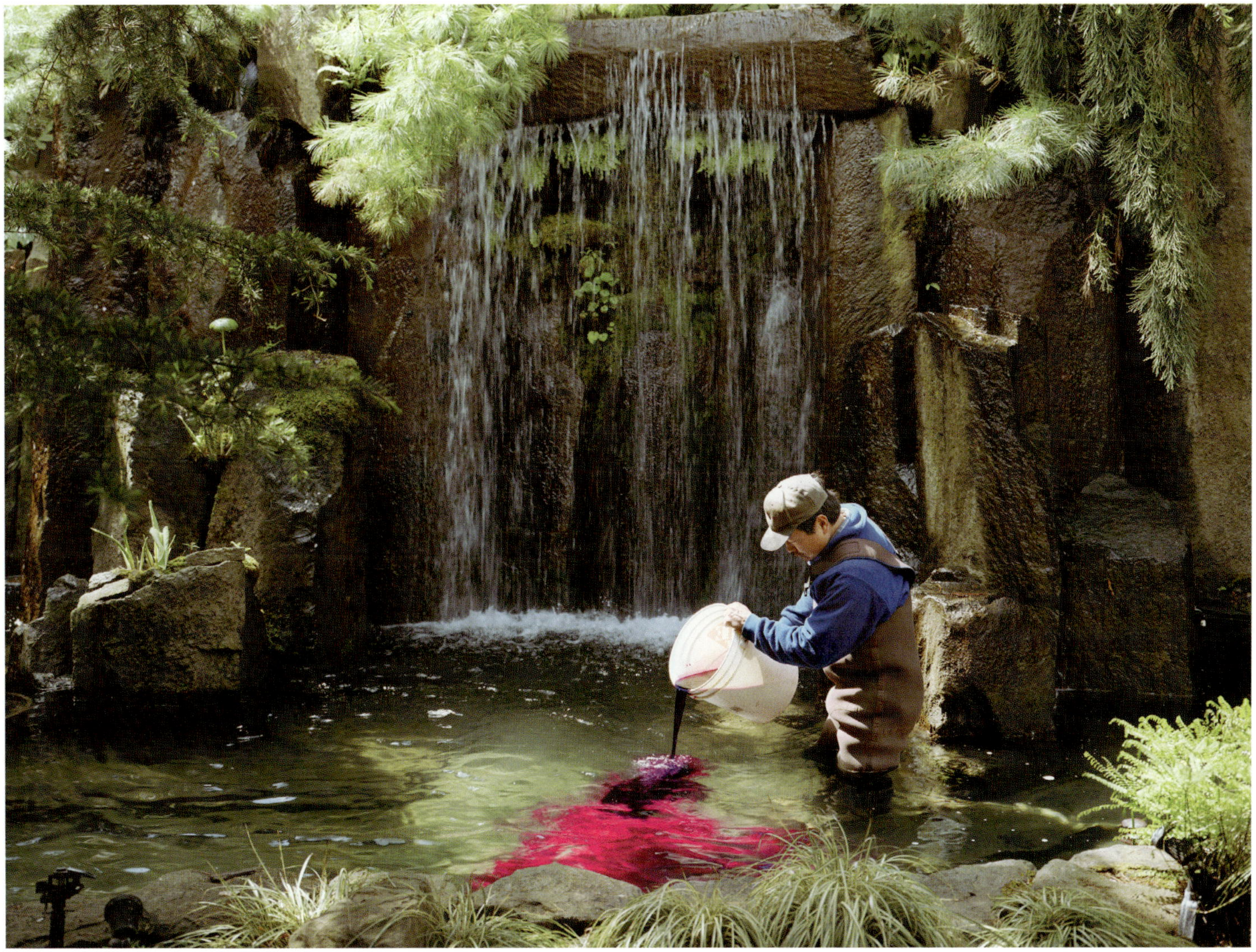

**1** Pouring, Ben Kubomiwa Treating Fountain with Potassium Permanganate 2002

**1** Verser, Ben Kubomiwa traite la fontaine avec du permanganate de potassium 2002

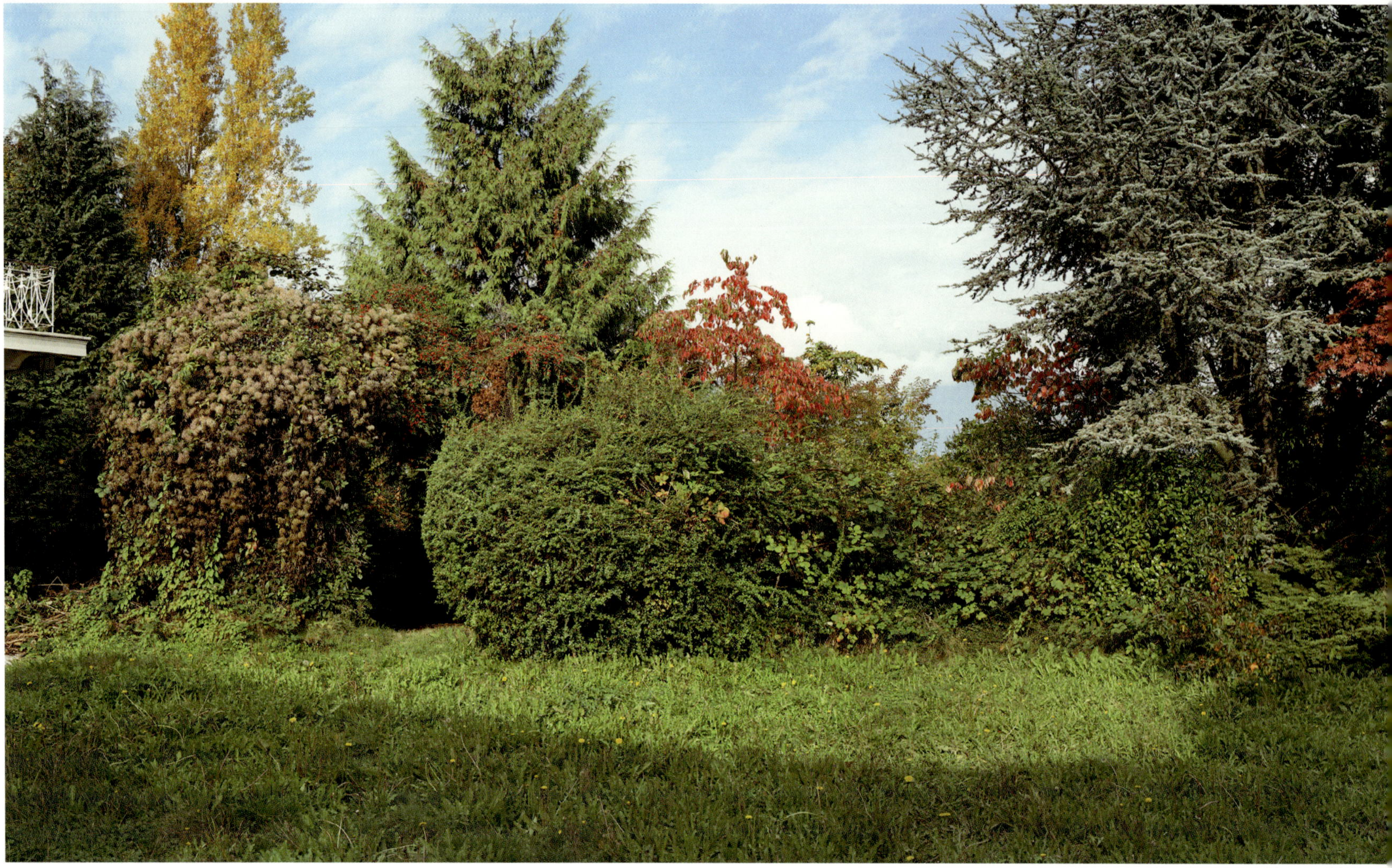

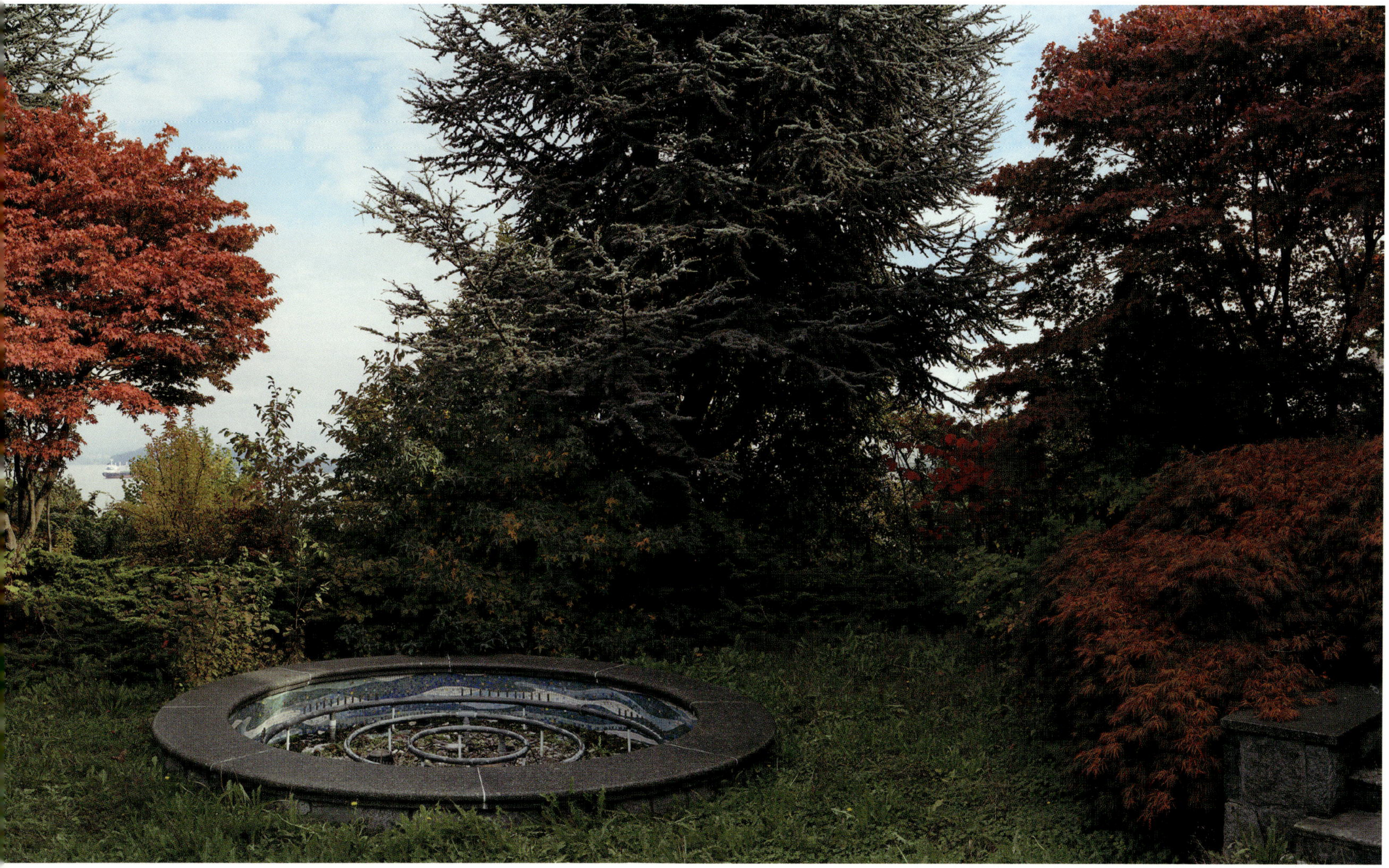

**2** Fountain Study, Late Fall; Cedrus atlantica, Acer palmatum, Populus nigra 2004

**2** Étude d'une fontaine, à la fin de l'automne. Cedrus atlantica, Acer palmatum, Populus nigra 2004

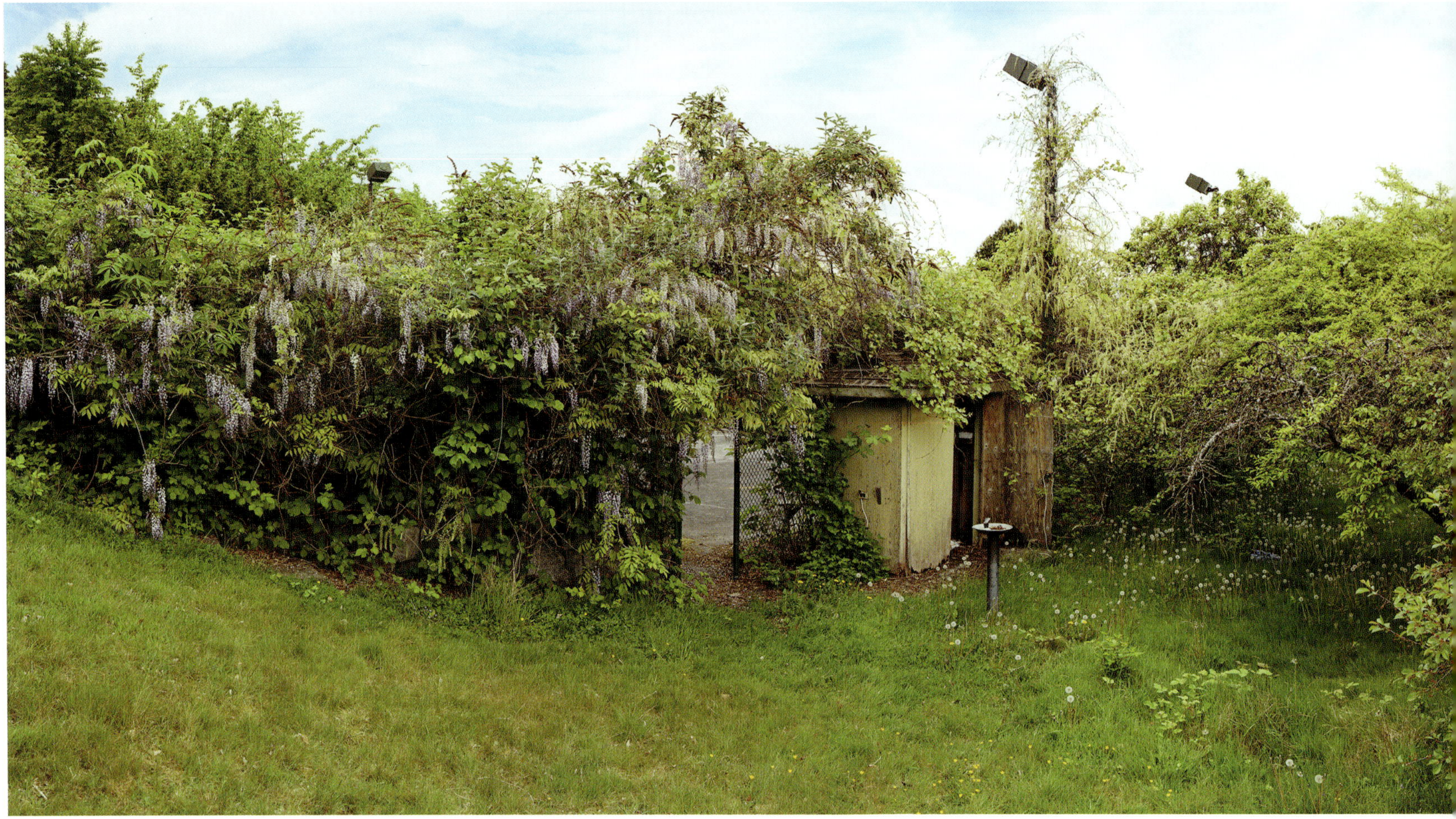

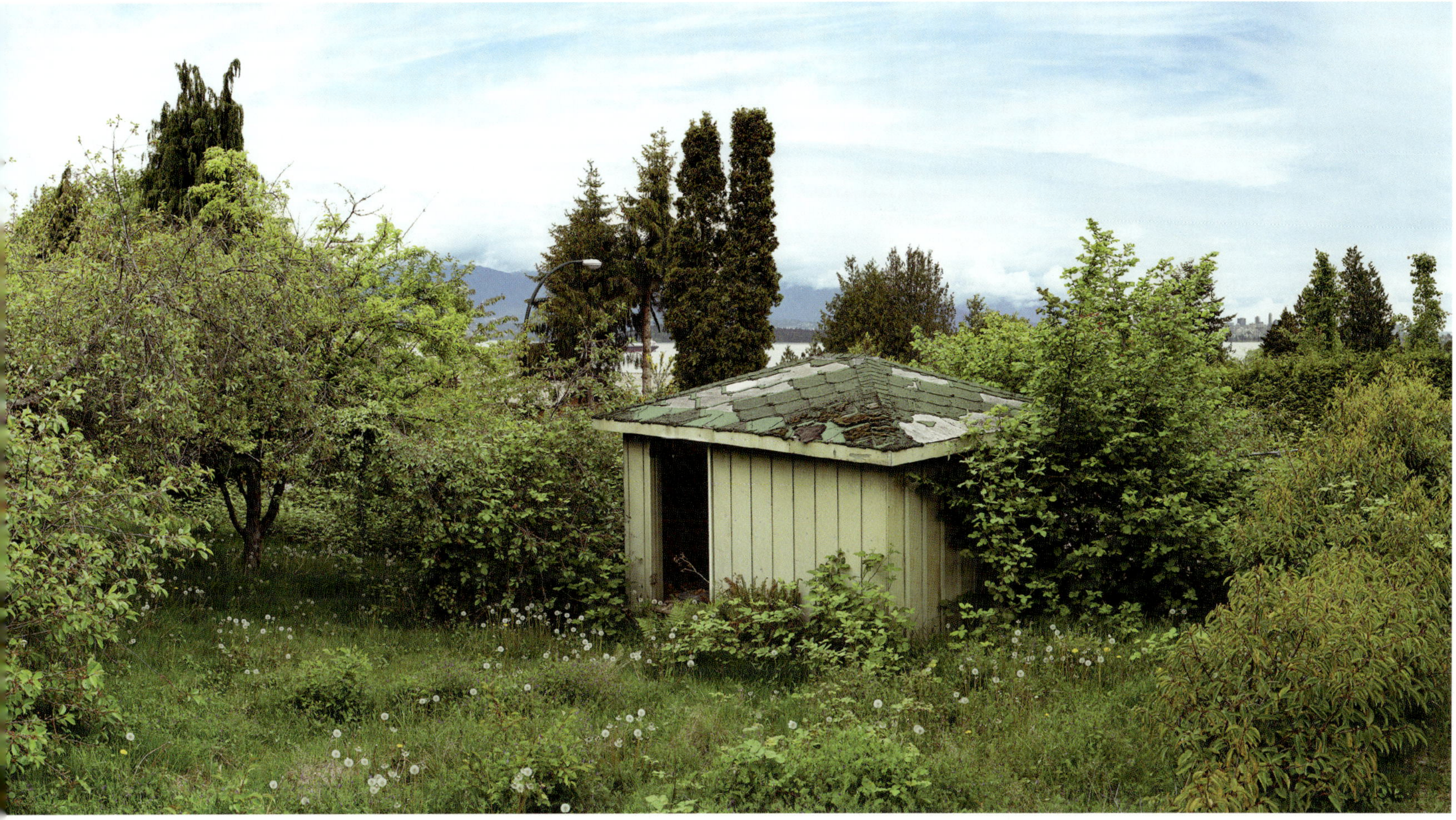

**3** Orchard View, Late Spring; Vitis vinifera, Wisteria 2004

**3** Vue d'un verger, à la fin du printemps. Vitis vinifera, Wisteria 2004

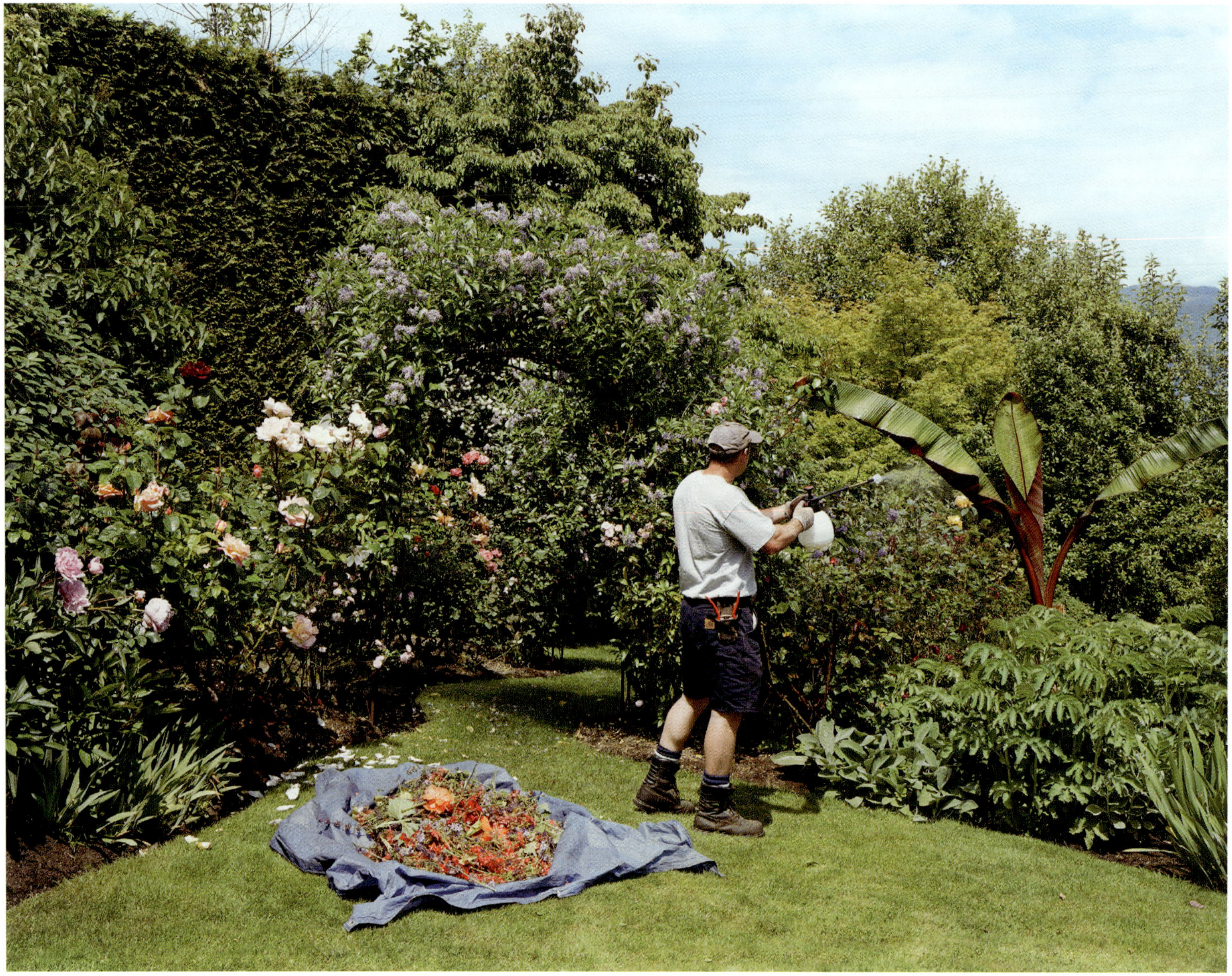

**4** Spraying, Norman Whaley Applying Aphid Solution 2004

**4** Pulvériser, Norman Whaley applique un aphicide 2004

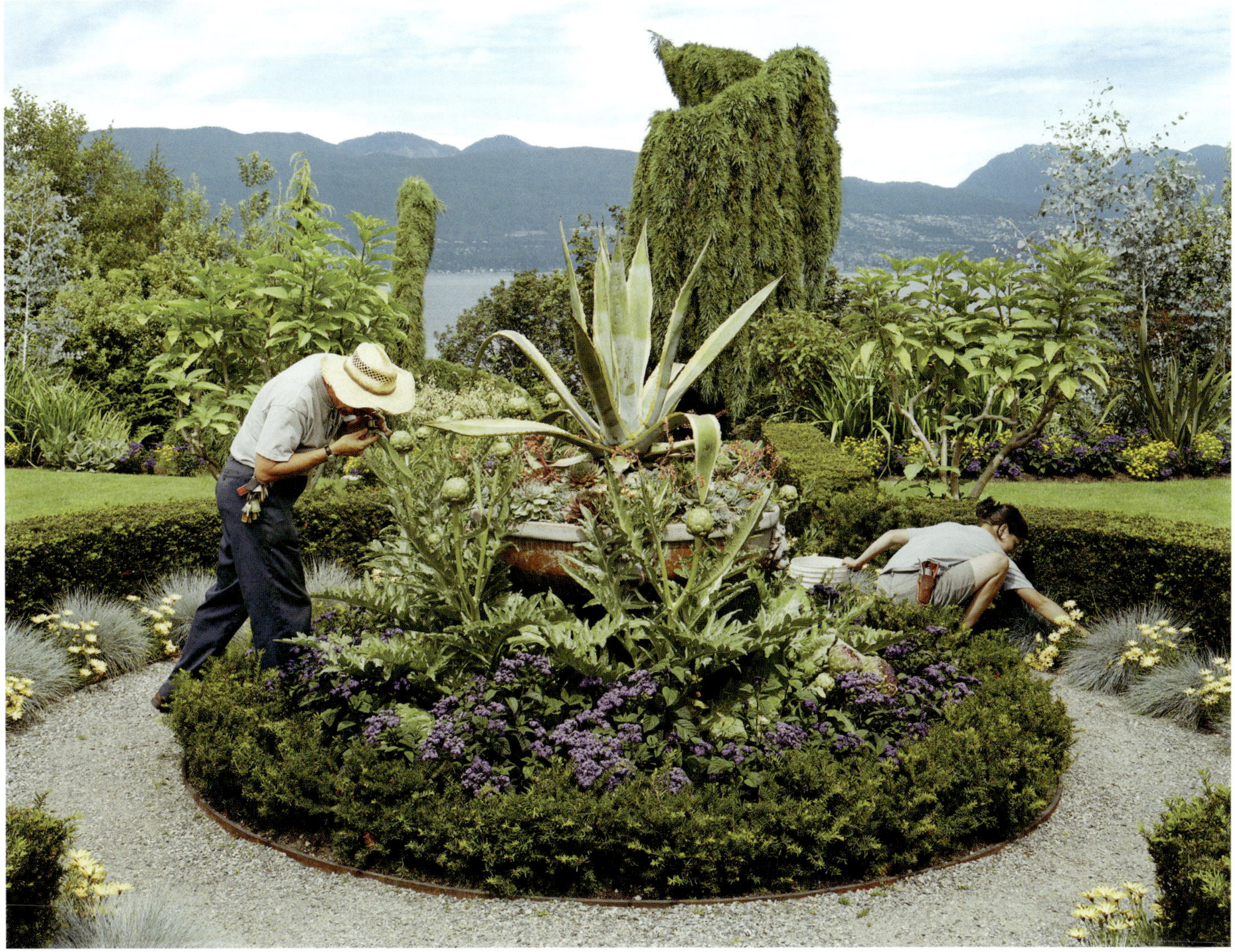

**5** **Inspecting, Allan O'Connor Searches for Botrytis cinerea** 2003

5 Inspecter, Allan O'Connor cherche du Botrytis cinerea 2003

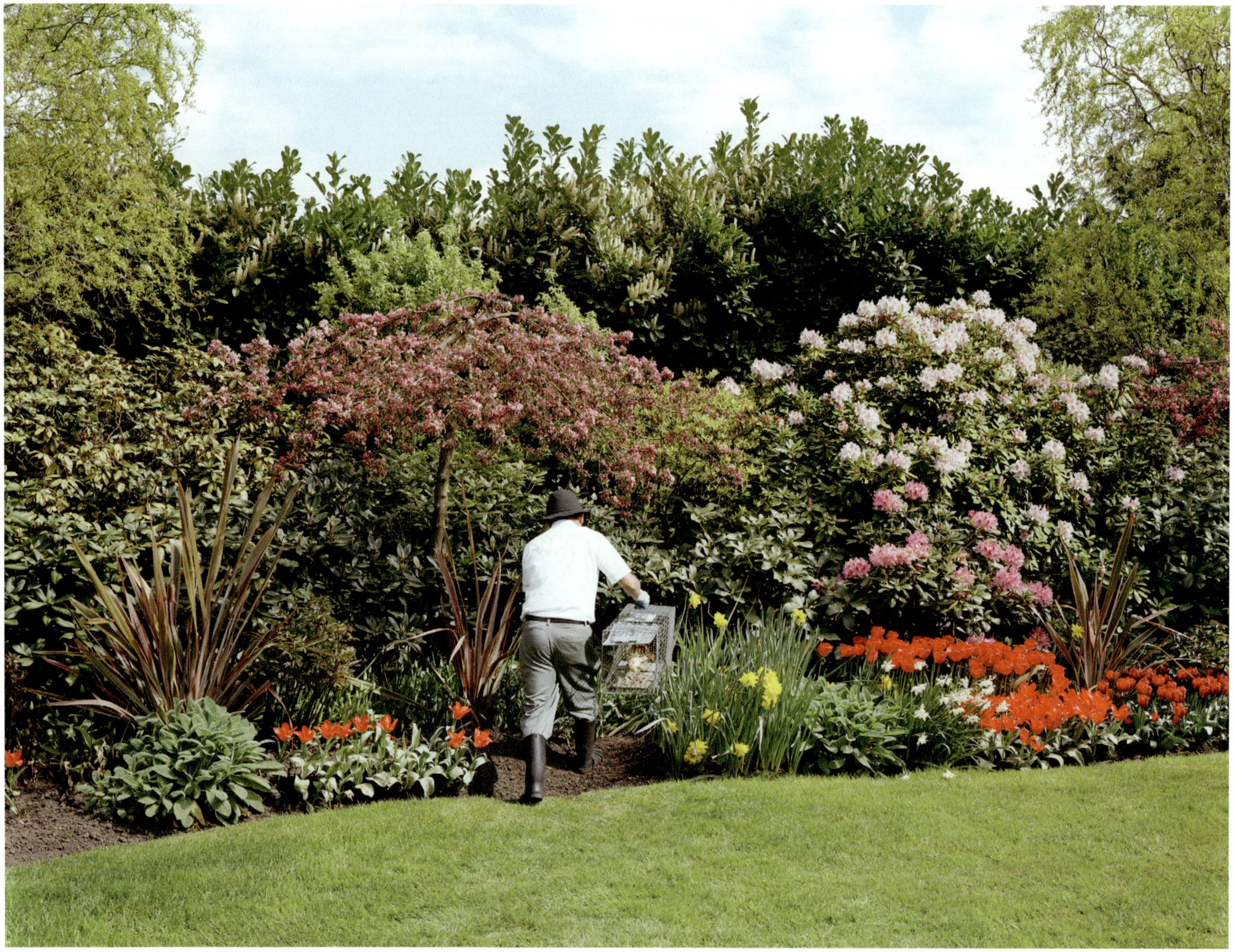

**6** Trapping, Ernesto Gacutan Positions Against Fauna 2003

**6** Piéger, Ernesto Gacutan met en place un piège contre la faune 2003

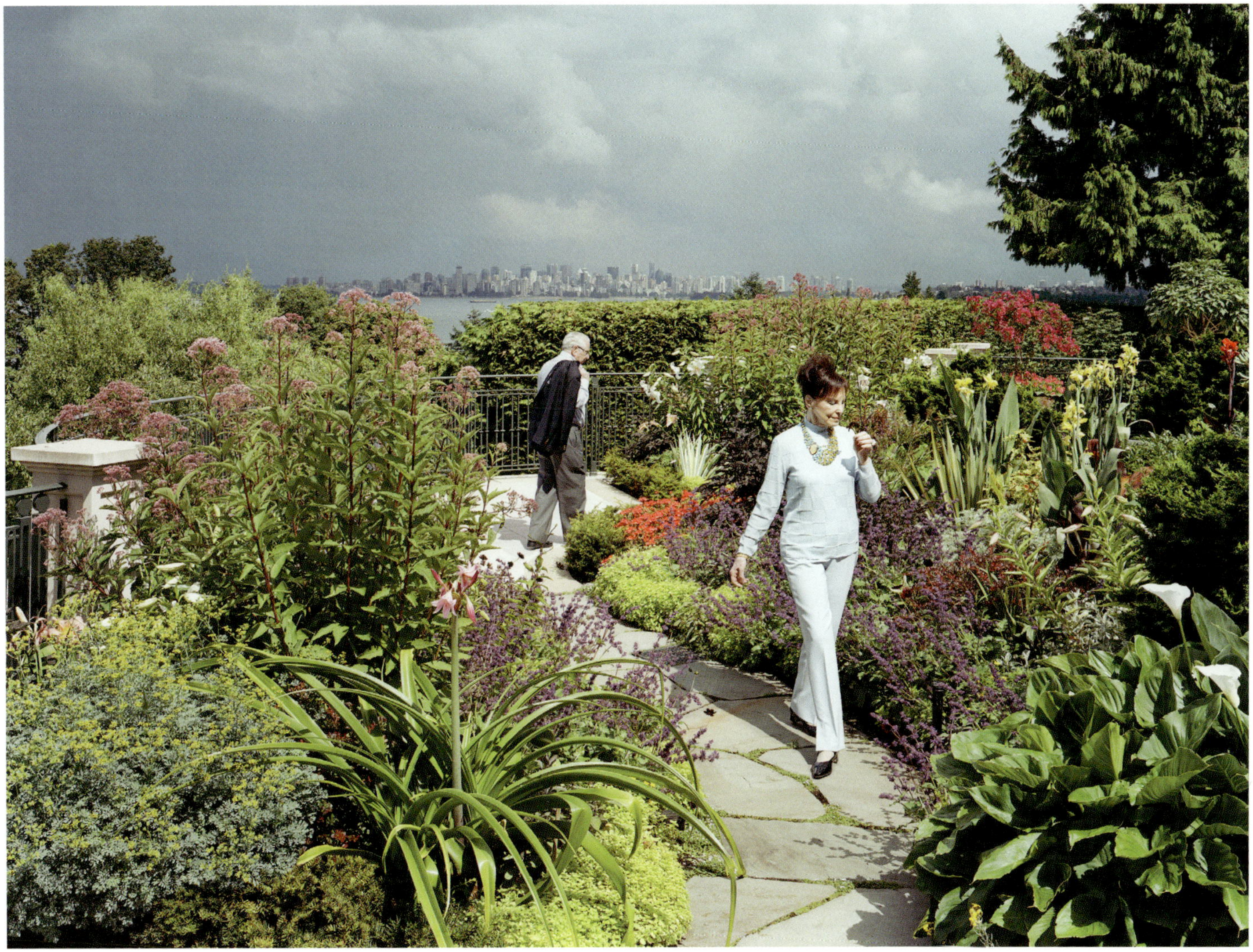

**7** On the Terrace Garden, Joe and Rosalee Segal with Cosmos atrosanguineus 2004

**7** Dans le jardin de la terrasse, Joe et Rosalee Segal avec du Cosmos atrosanguineus 2004

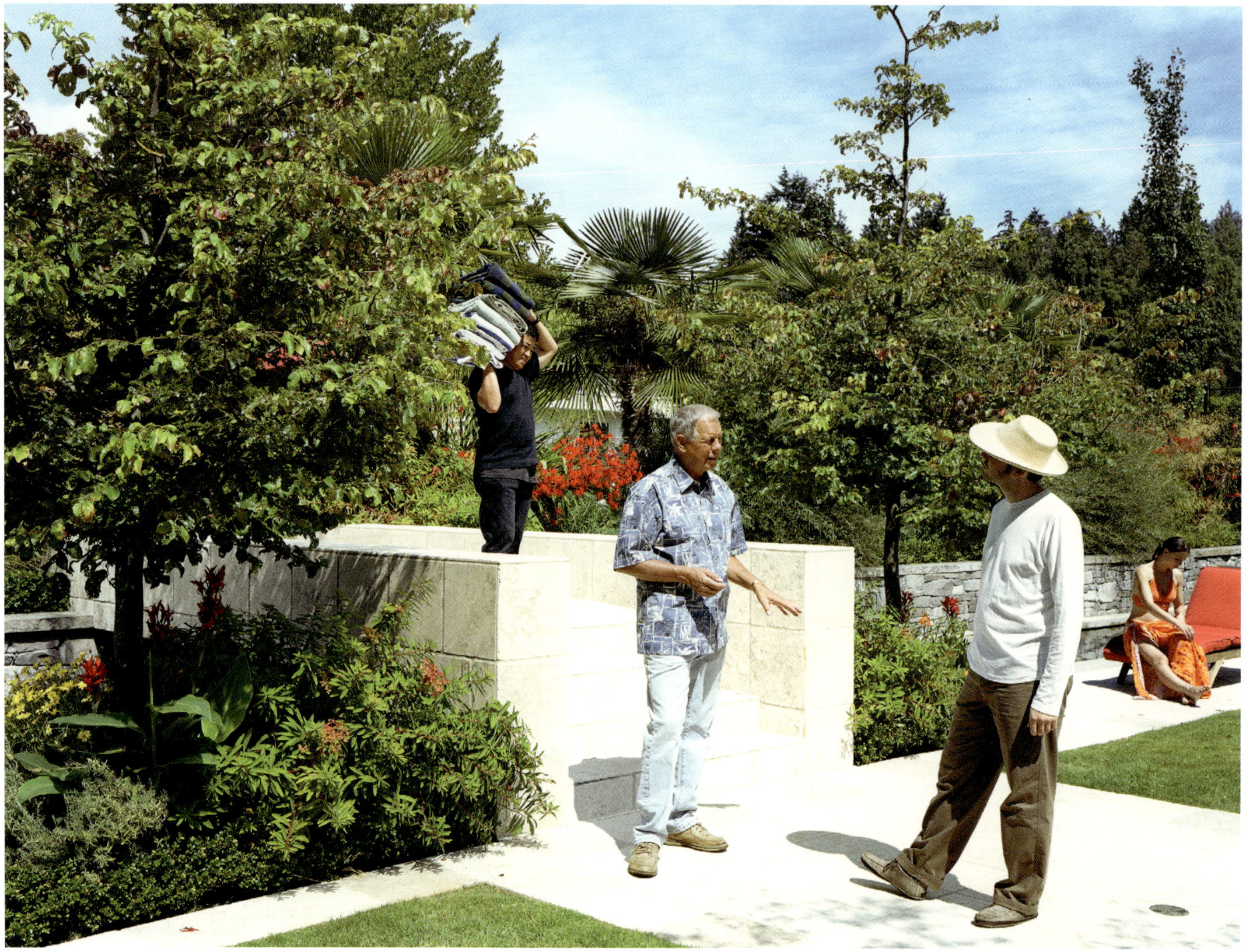

**8** Discussing, Michael O'Brian with Artist and Model on his Property 2005

**8** Discuter, Michael O'Brian avec artiste et modèle sur sa propriété 2005

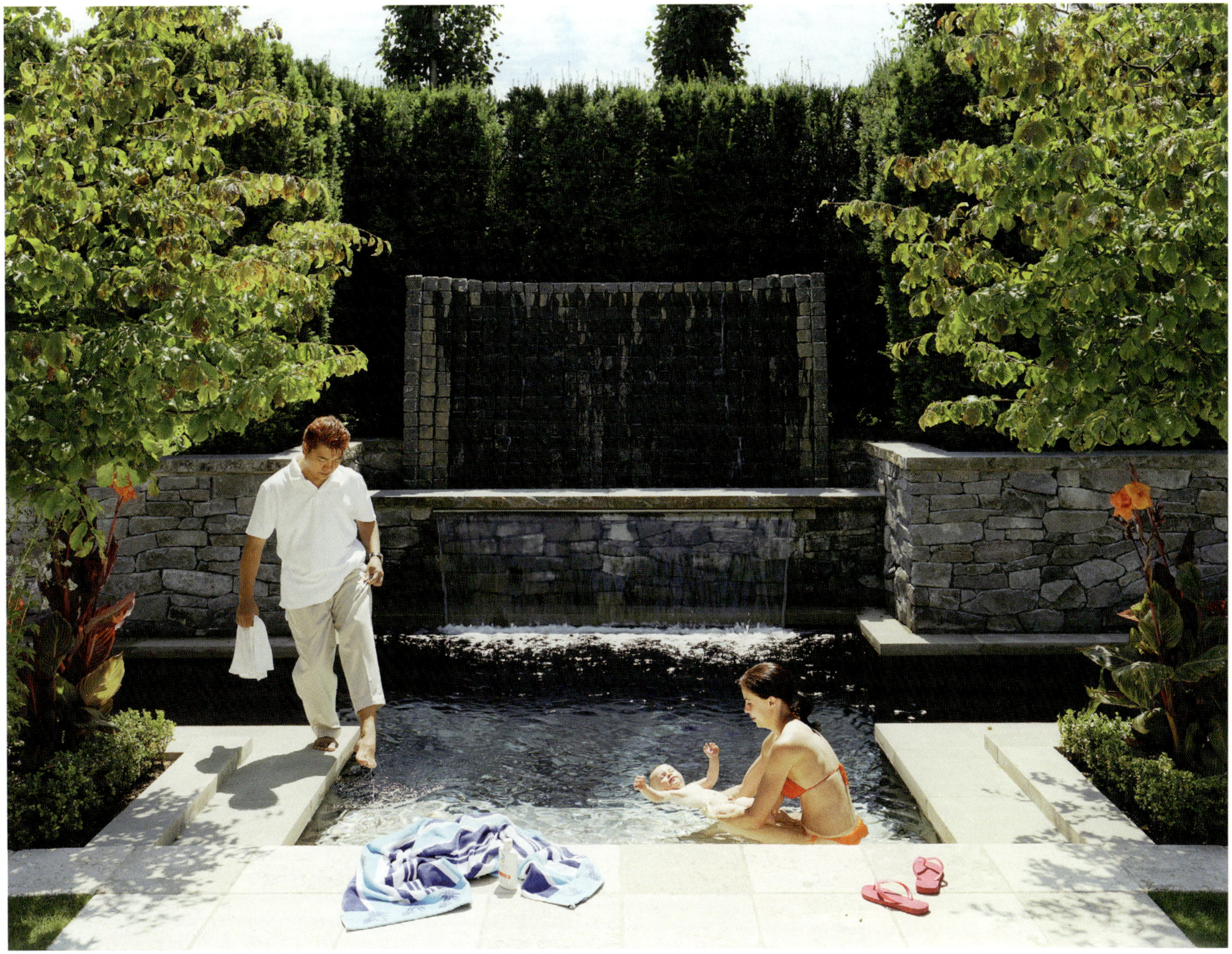

**9** Dipping, Conrad Arida with Mother and Child Wading in the Water 2004

**9** Baigner, Conrad Arida avec mère et enfant pataugeant dans l'eau 2004

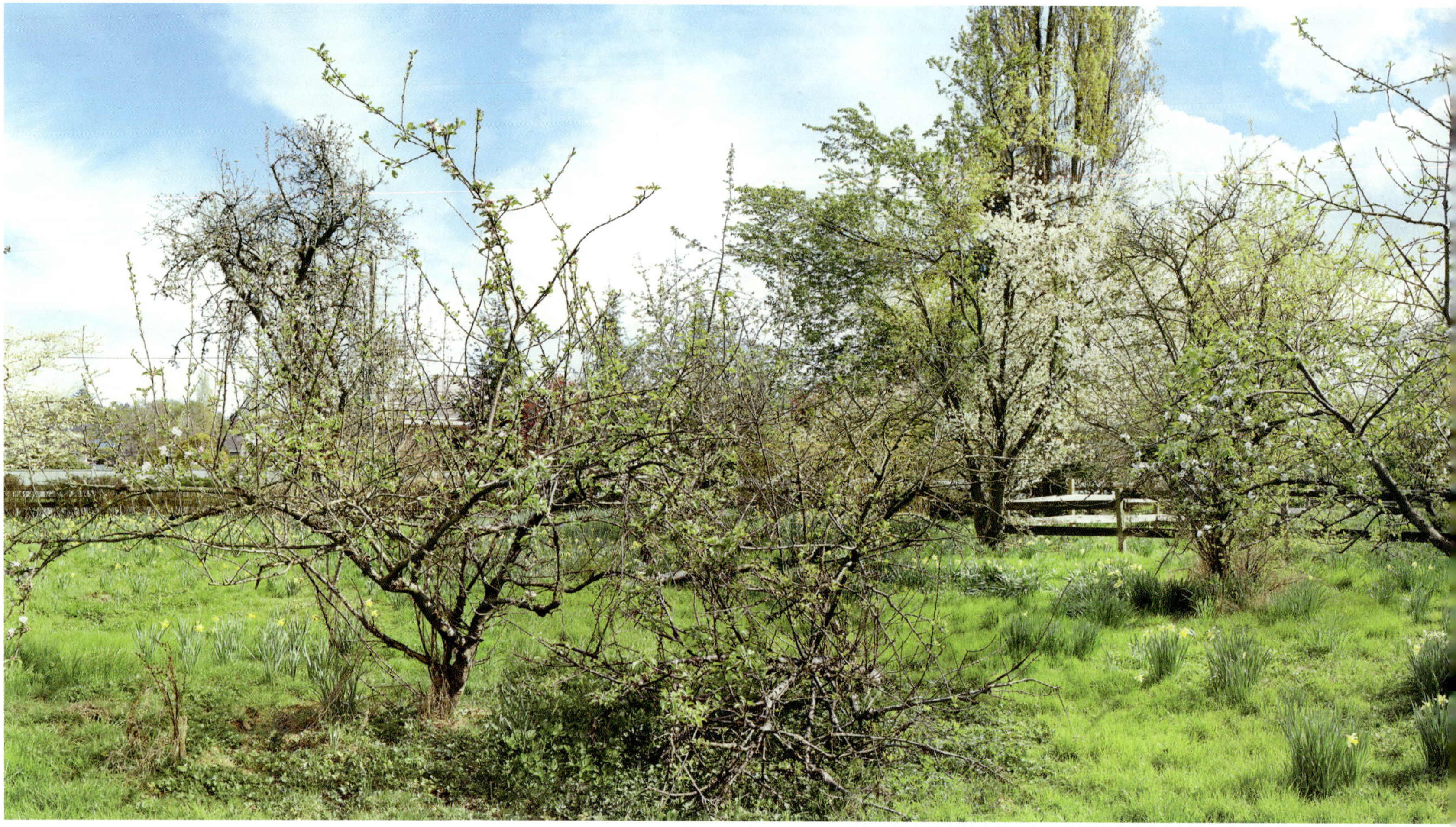

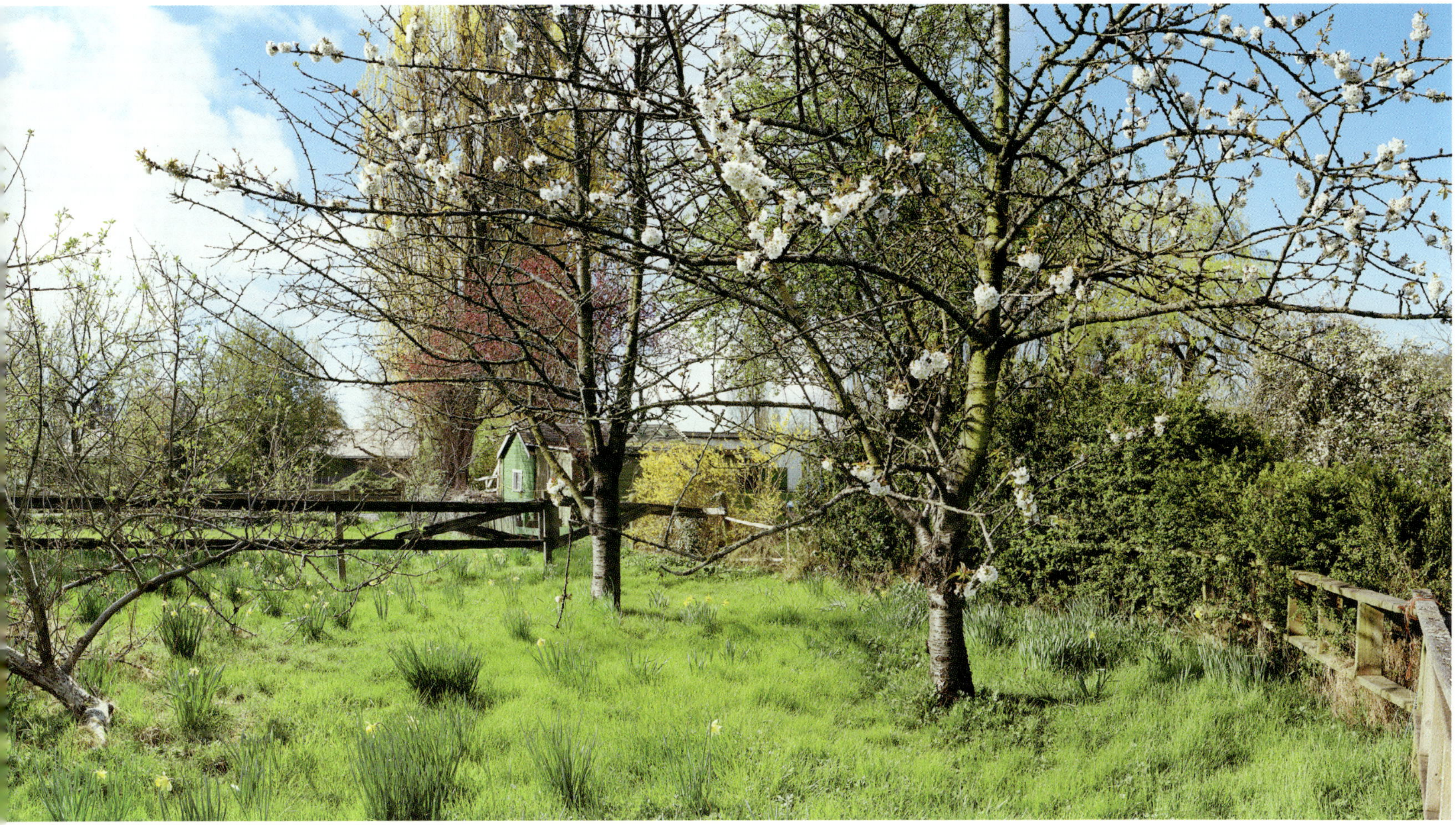

**10** Orchard on Dr. Young's Property, 3226 W. 51st. Vancouver 2005

**10** Verger de la propriété du D^r^ Young, 3226, 51^e^ rue O., Vancouver 2005

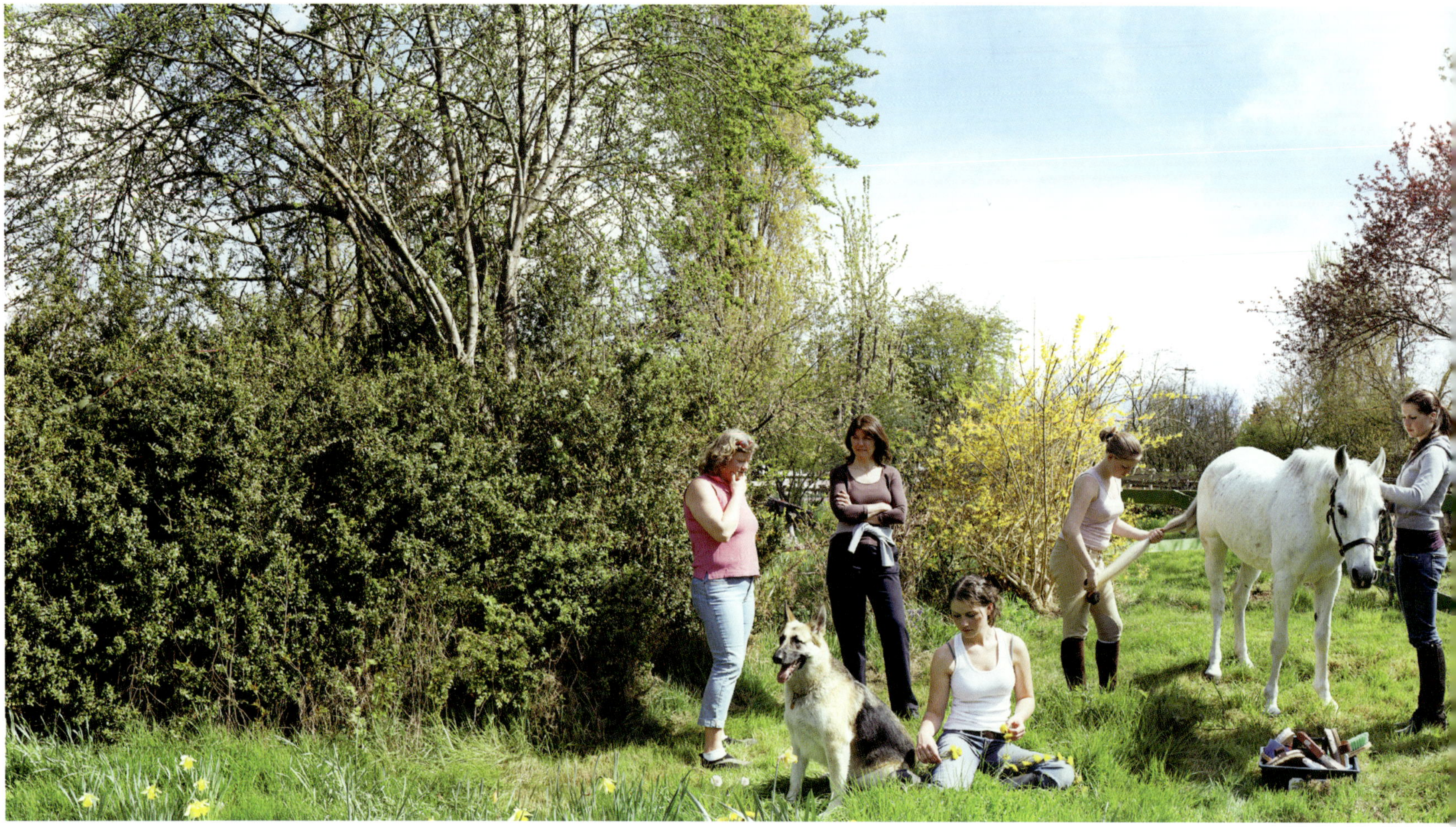

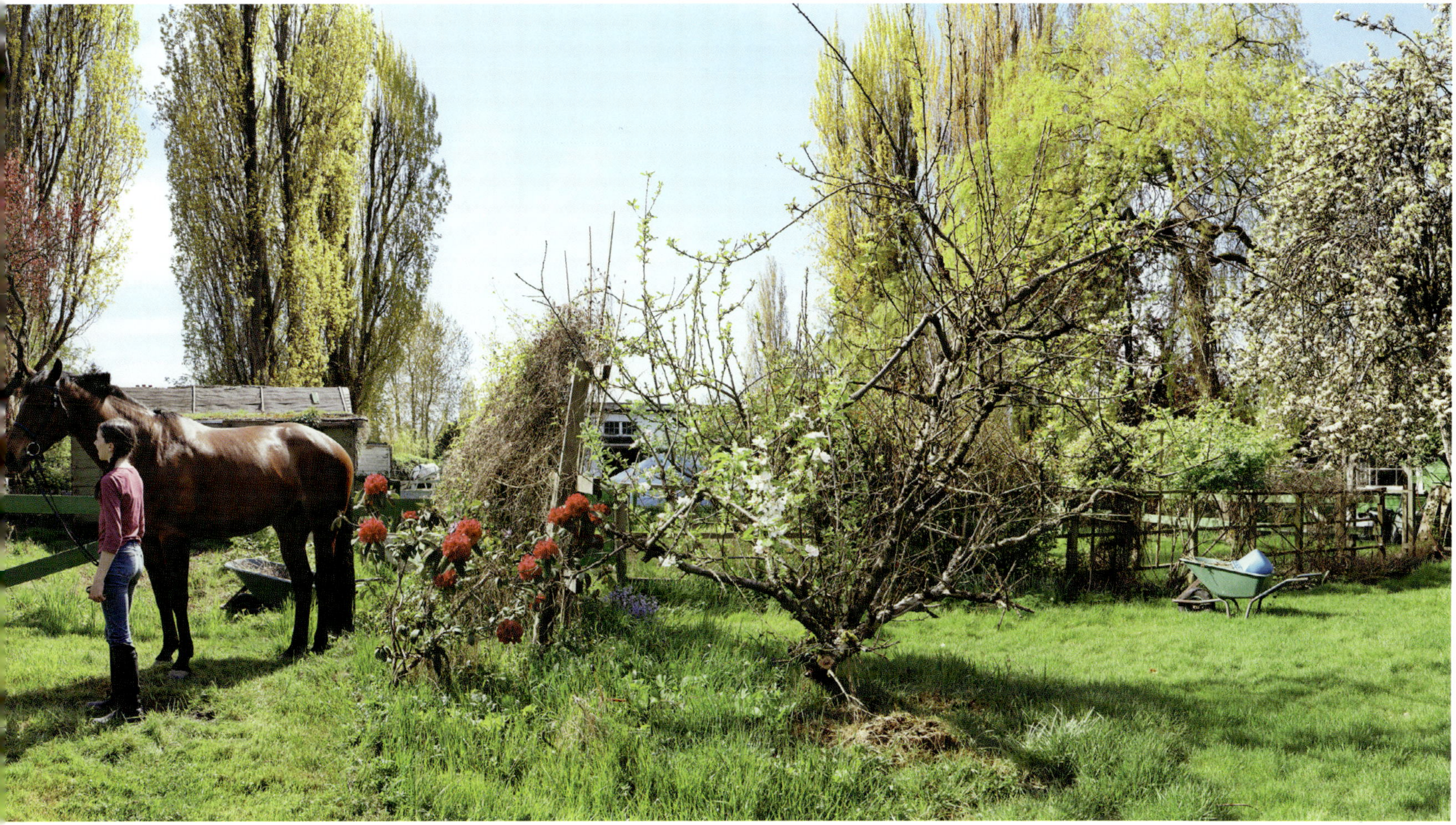

**11** Stables on Dr. Young's Property, 3226 W. 51st. Vancouver 2005

**11** Écuries de la propriété du D$^{r}$ Young, 3226, 51$^{e}$ rue O., Vancouver 2005

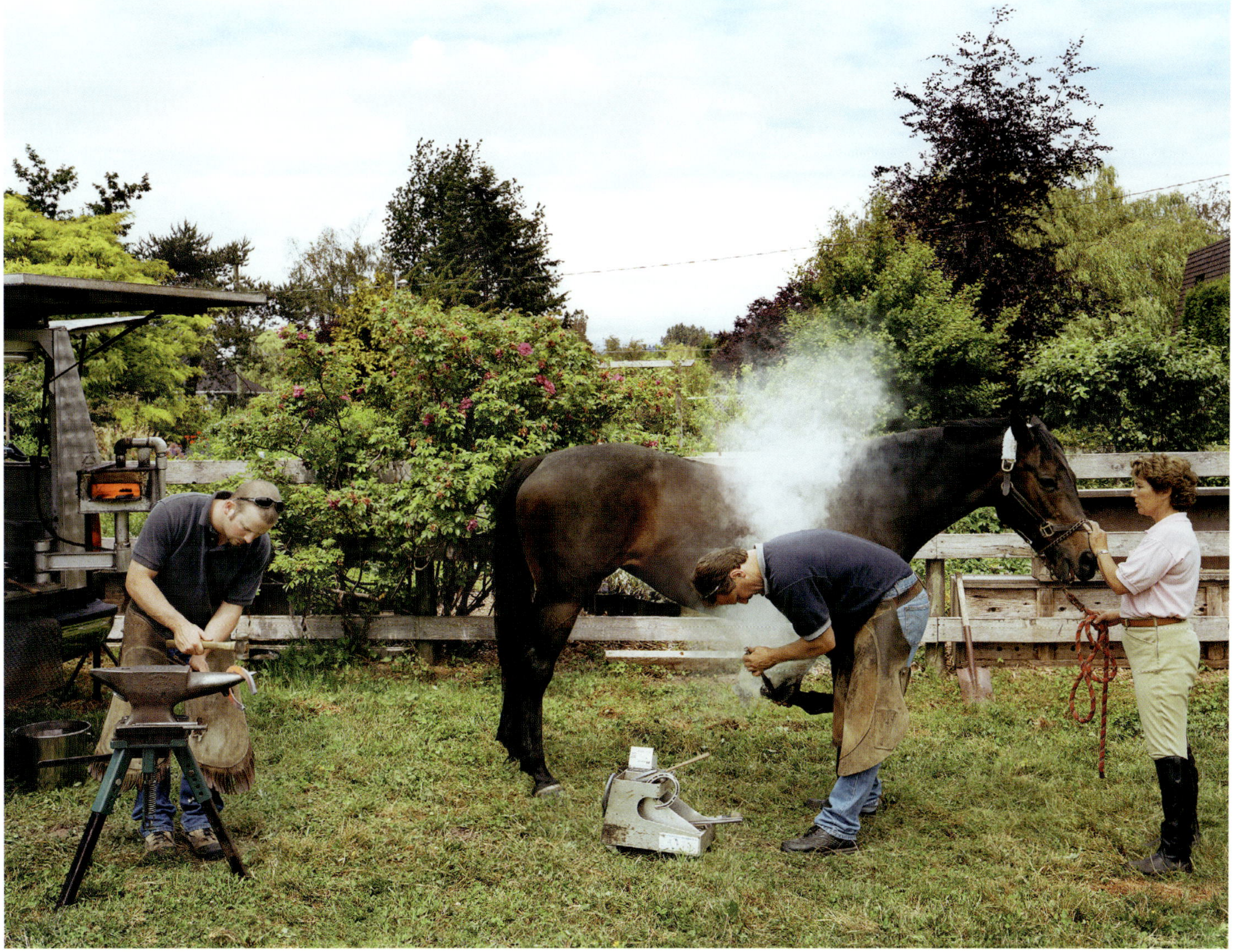

**12** Reshoeing, Ferrier James Findel with Assistant on Southlands 2008

**12** Nouveau ferrage, le maréchal-ferrant James Findel avec son adjoint dans les Southlands 2008

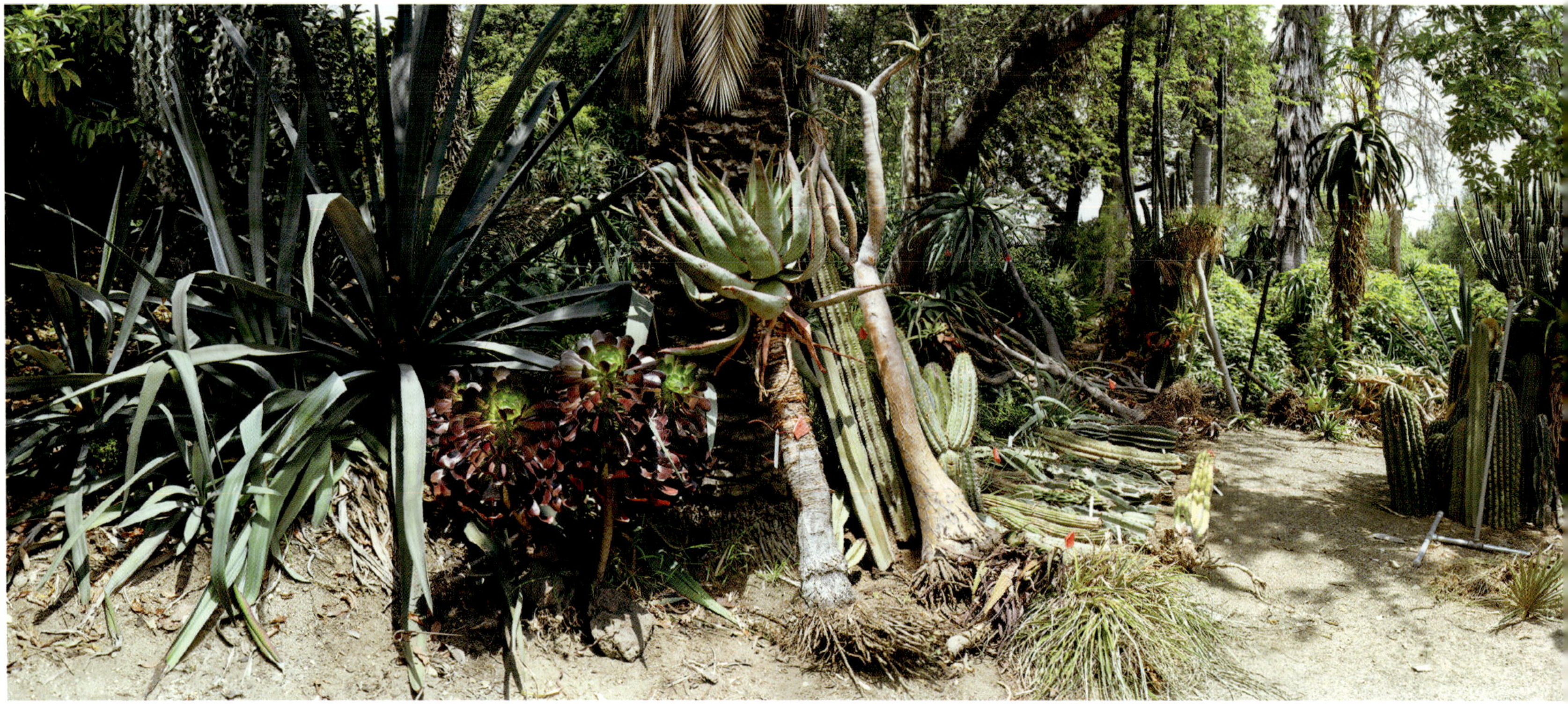

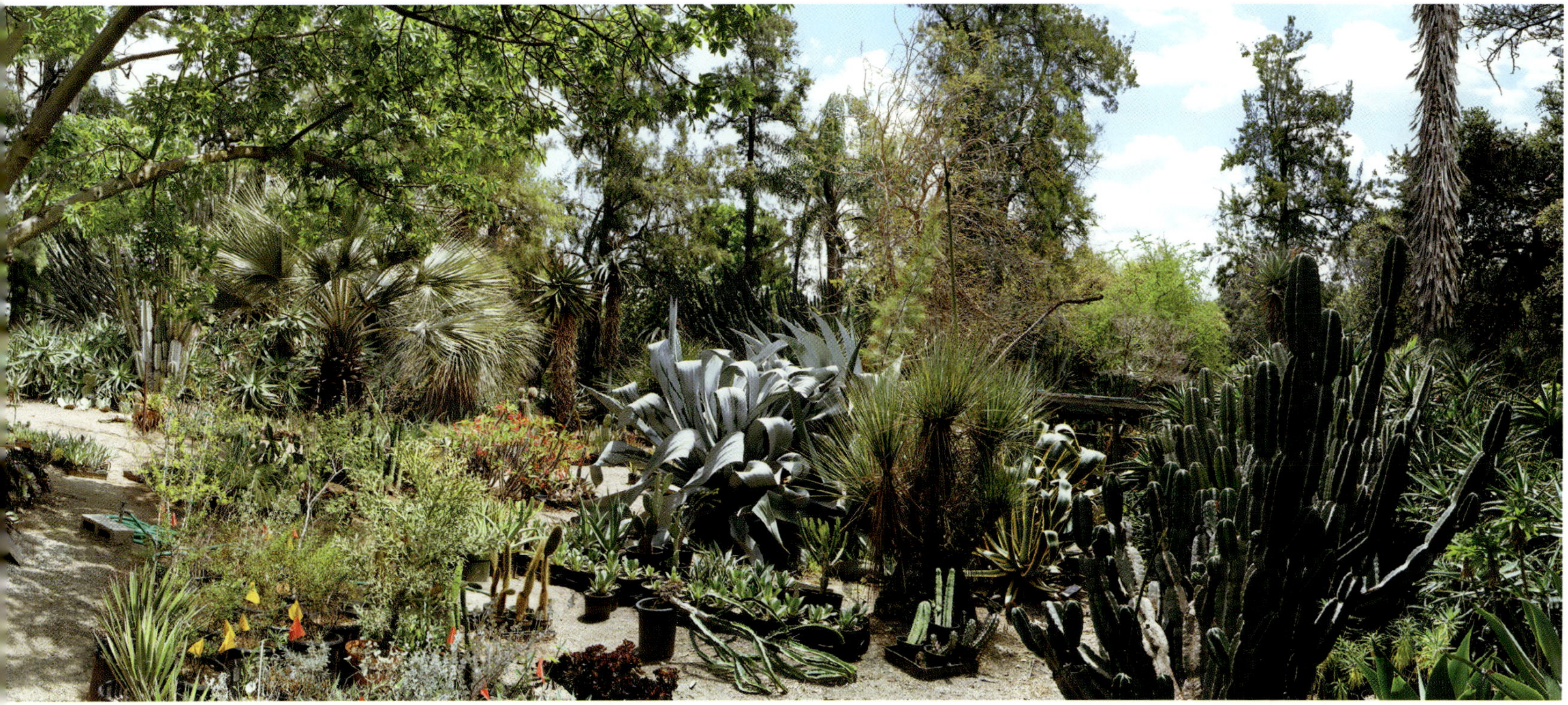

**13** Huntington Botanical Garden, San Marino, California. Desert Garden Nursery with Succulent Collections Donated by Virginia Martin and Seymour Lyndon, Spring 2005

**13** Huntington Botanical Garden, San Marino, Californie. Pépinière du jardin désertique avec les collections de plantes grasses données par Virginia Martin et Seymour Lyndon, printemps 2005

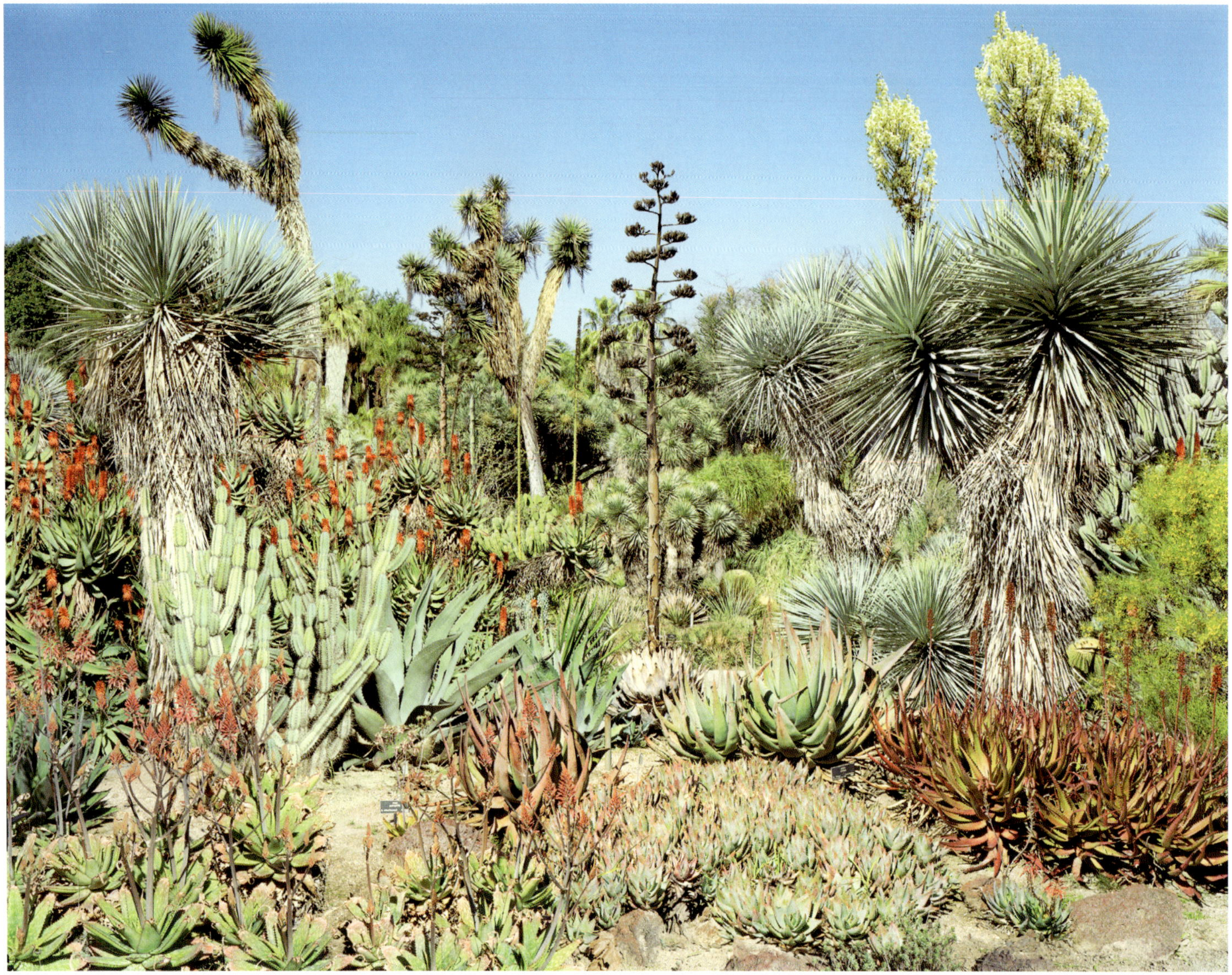

**14** Aloe principis 2006

**14** Aloe principis 2006

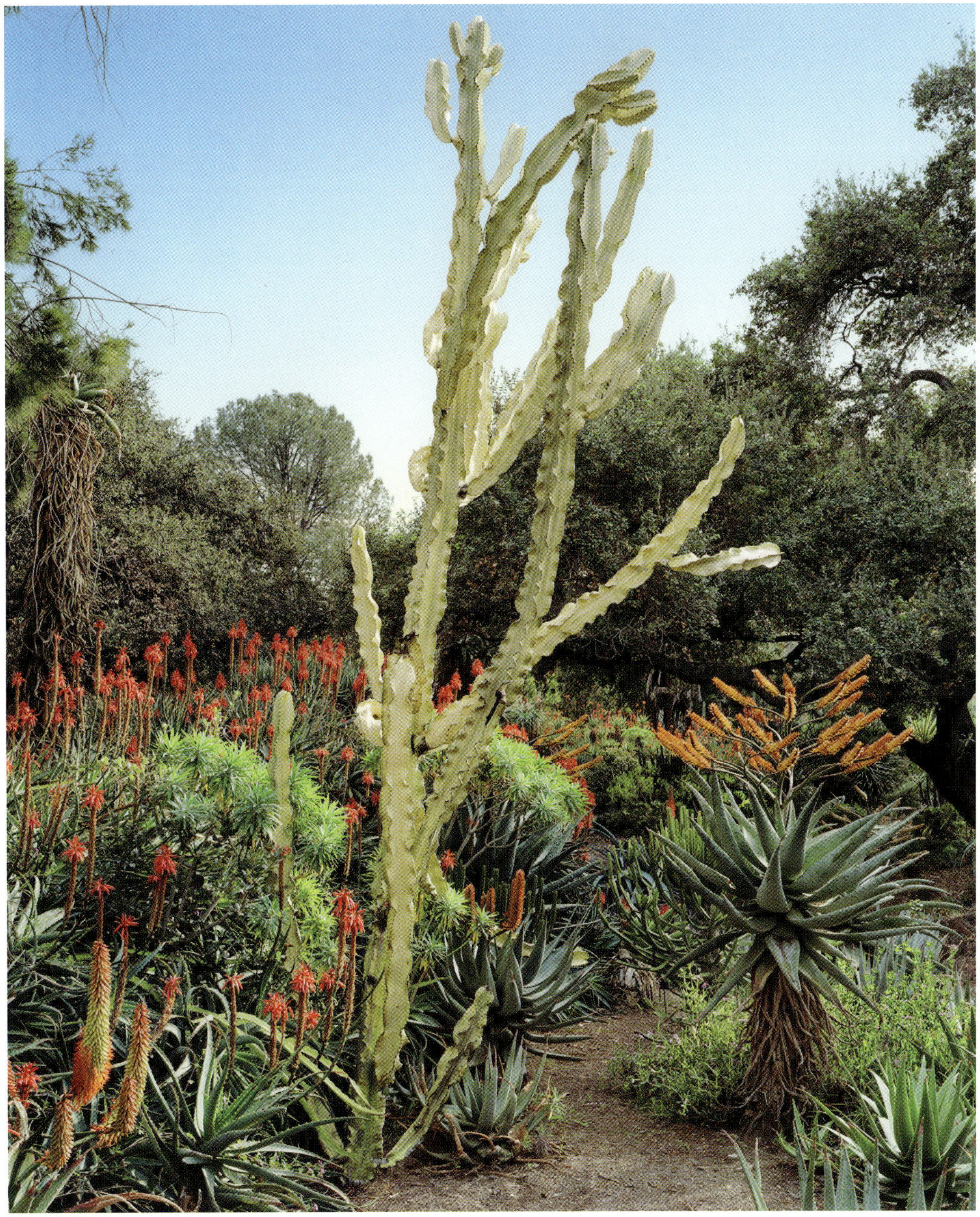

15 Euphorbia ingens 2006

15 Euphorbia ingens 2006

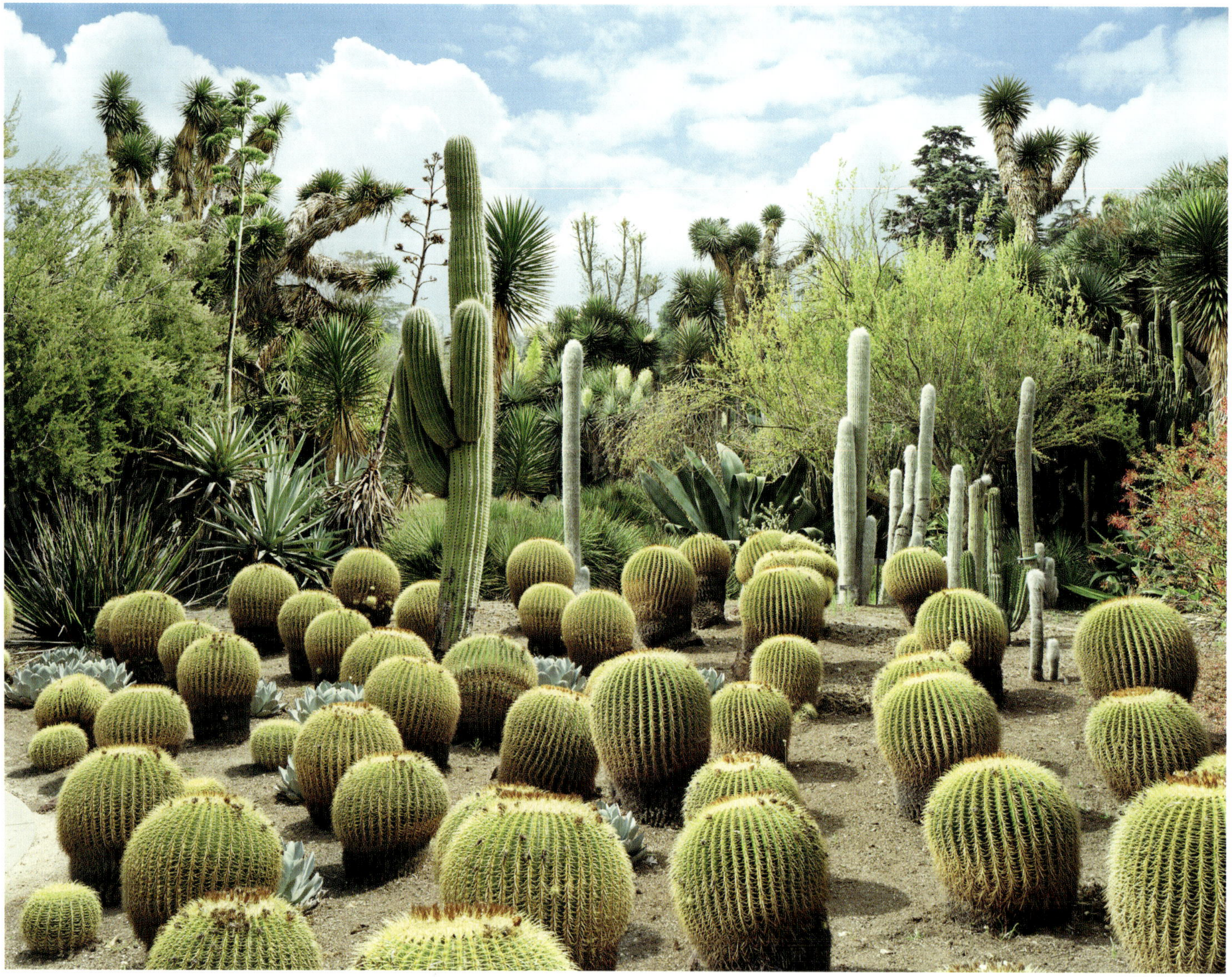

**16** Echinocactus grusonii 2006

**16** Echinocactus grusonii 2006

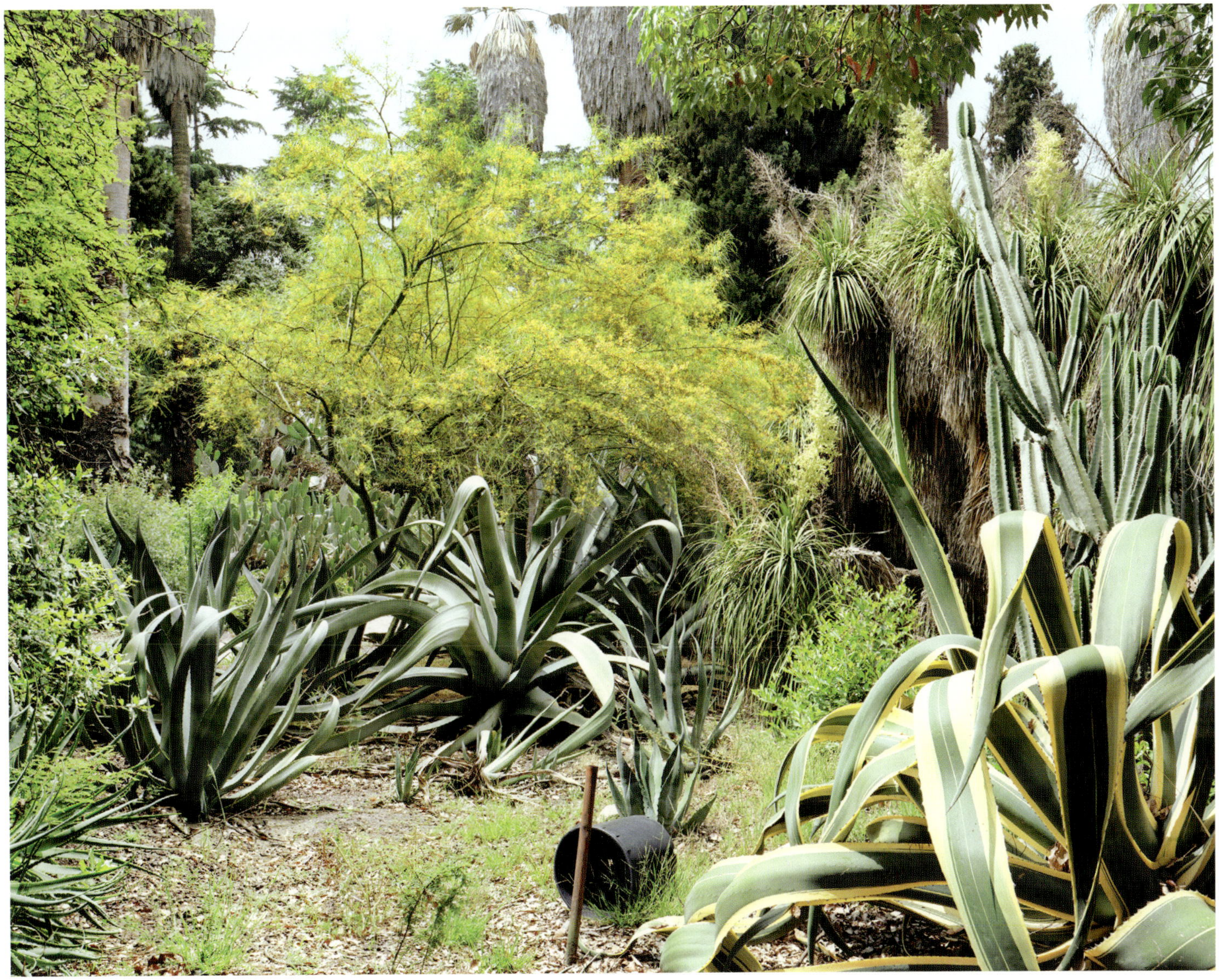

**17** Agave americana variegata 2006

**17** Agave americana variegata 2006

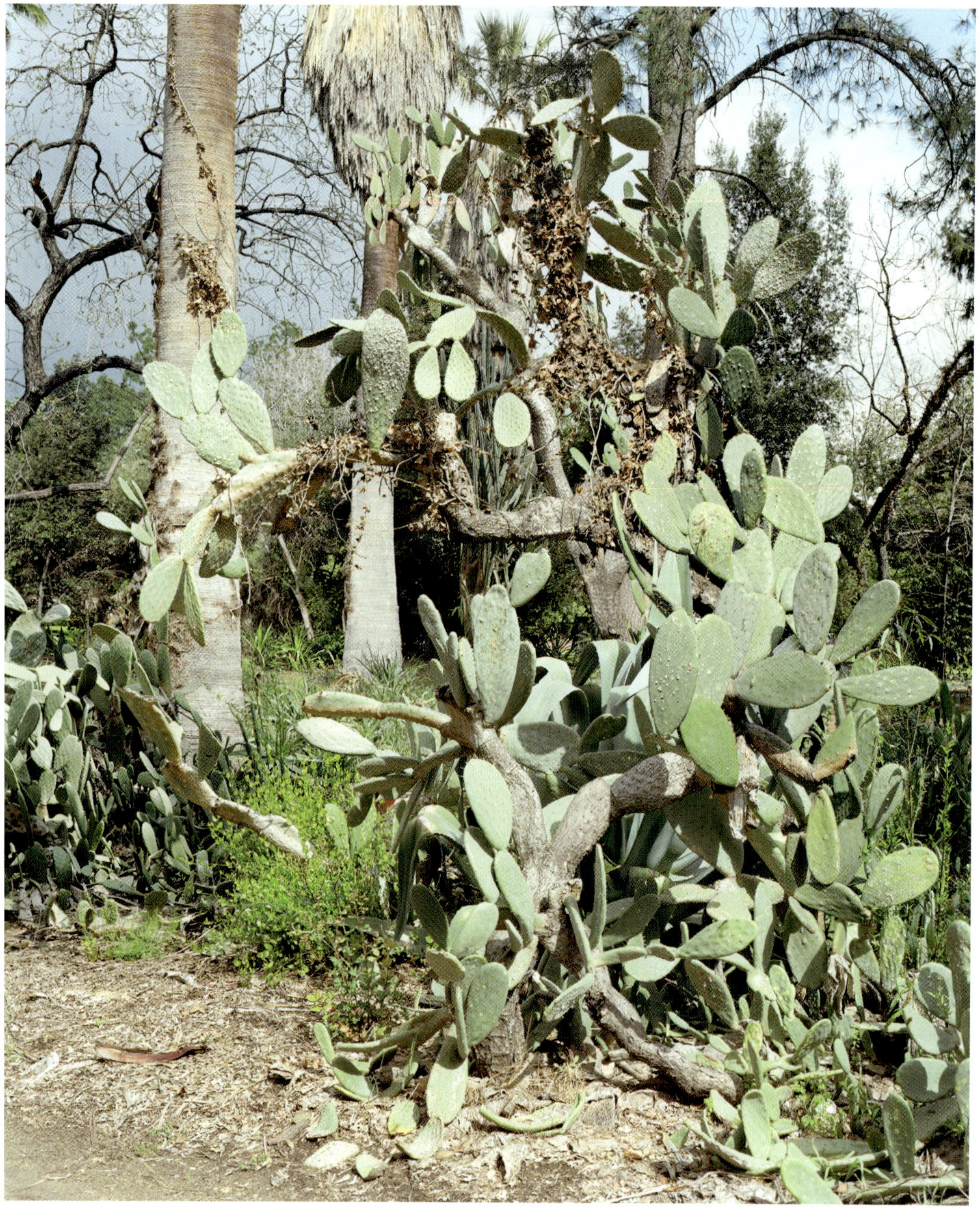

**18** Opuntia pittieri 2006

**18** Opuntia pittieri 2006

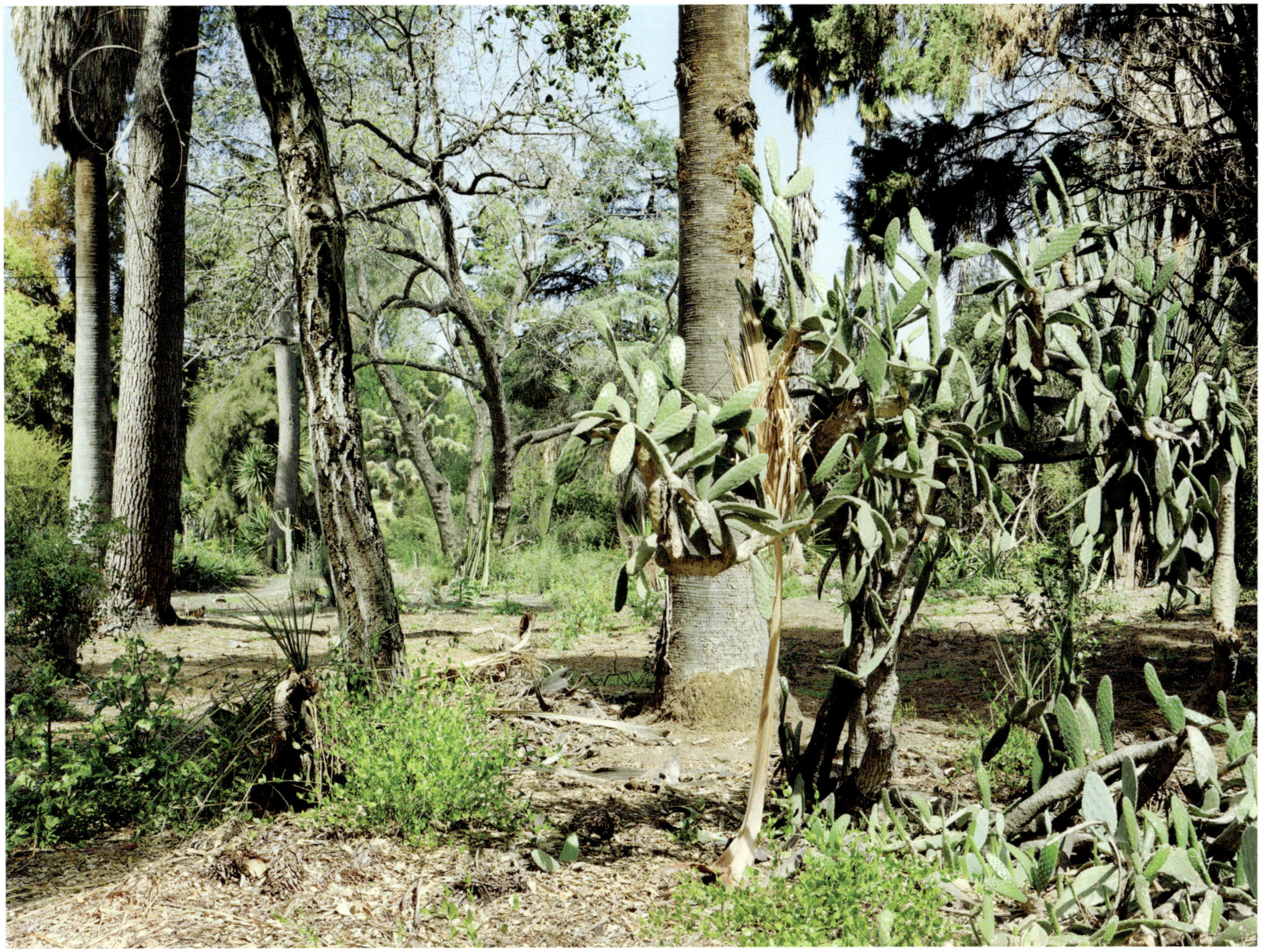

**19** Washingtonia filifera 2006

**19** Washingtonia filifera 2006

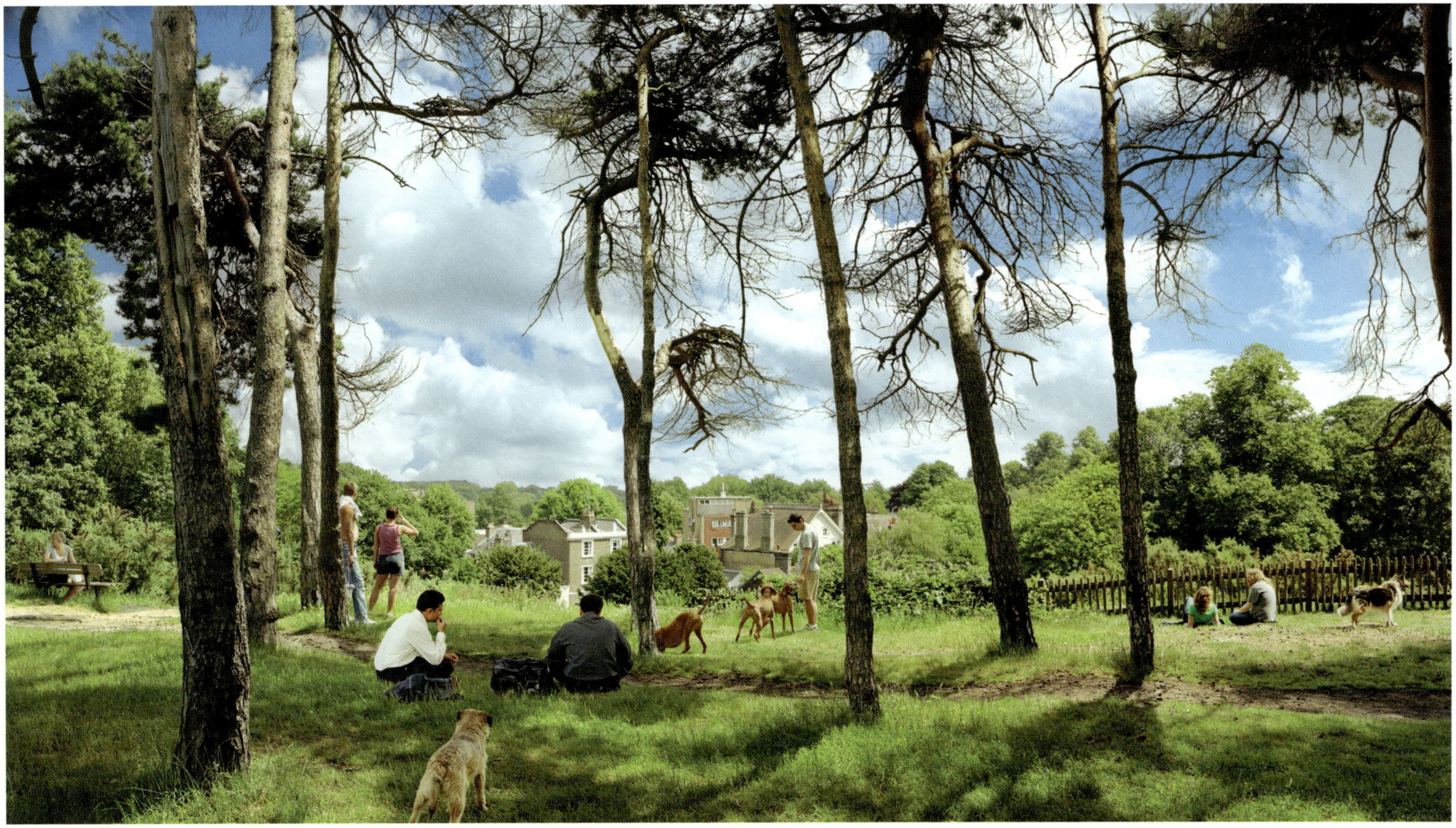

**20** View of Vale of Health, Looking Towards Hampstead (edition 1/5) 2007

**20** Vue de Vale of Health, vers Hampstead (édition 1/5) 2007

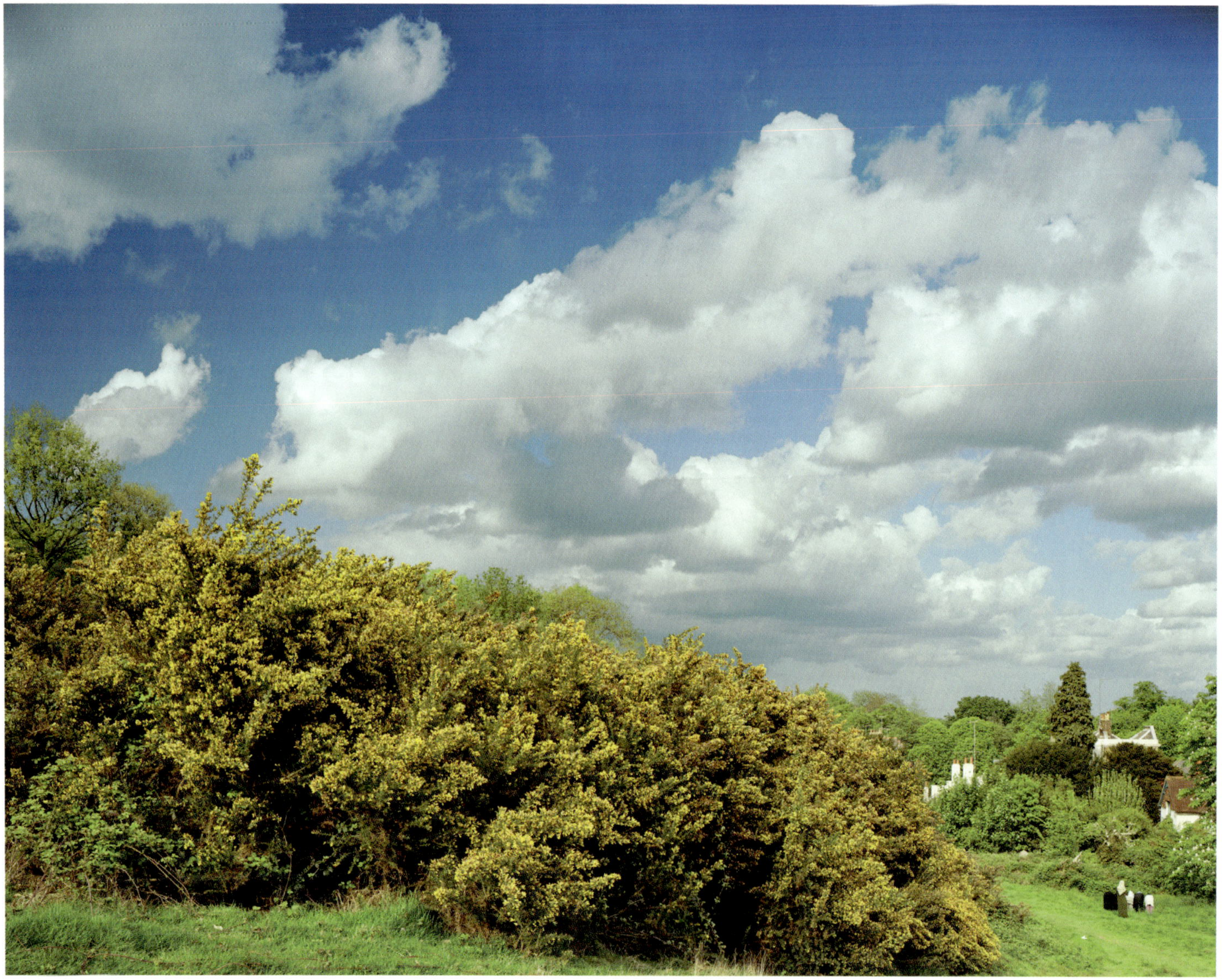

**21** Gorse and Sky (edition 2/5) 2008

**21** Ajonc et ciel (édition 2/5) 2008

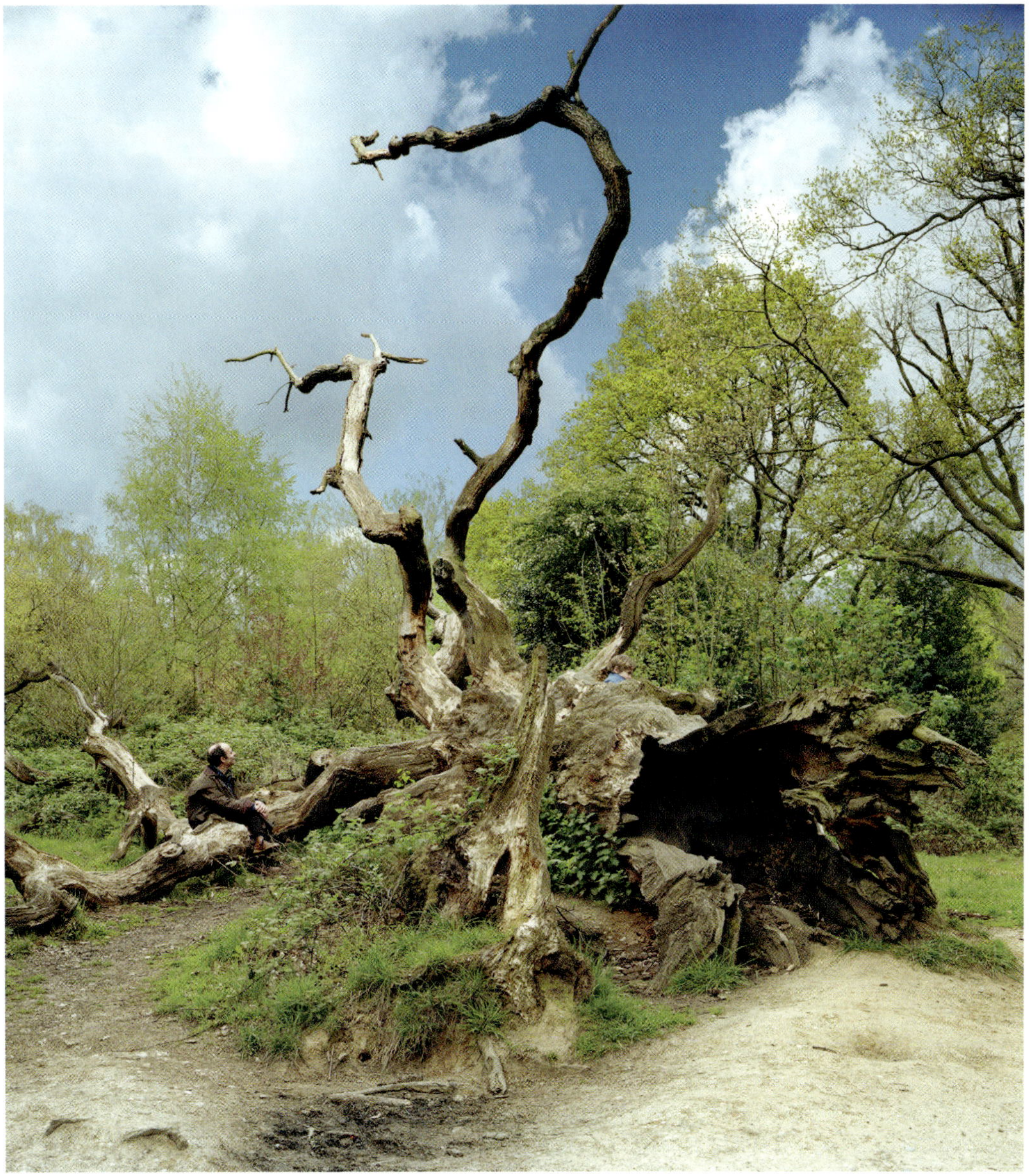

**22** Fallen Oak Tree (edition 2/5) 2008

**22** Chêne mort (édition 2/5) 2008

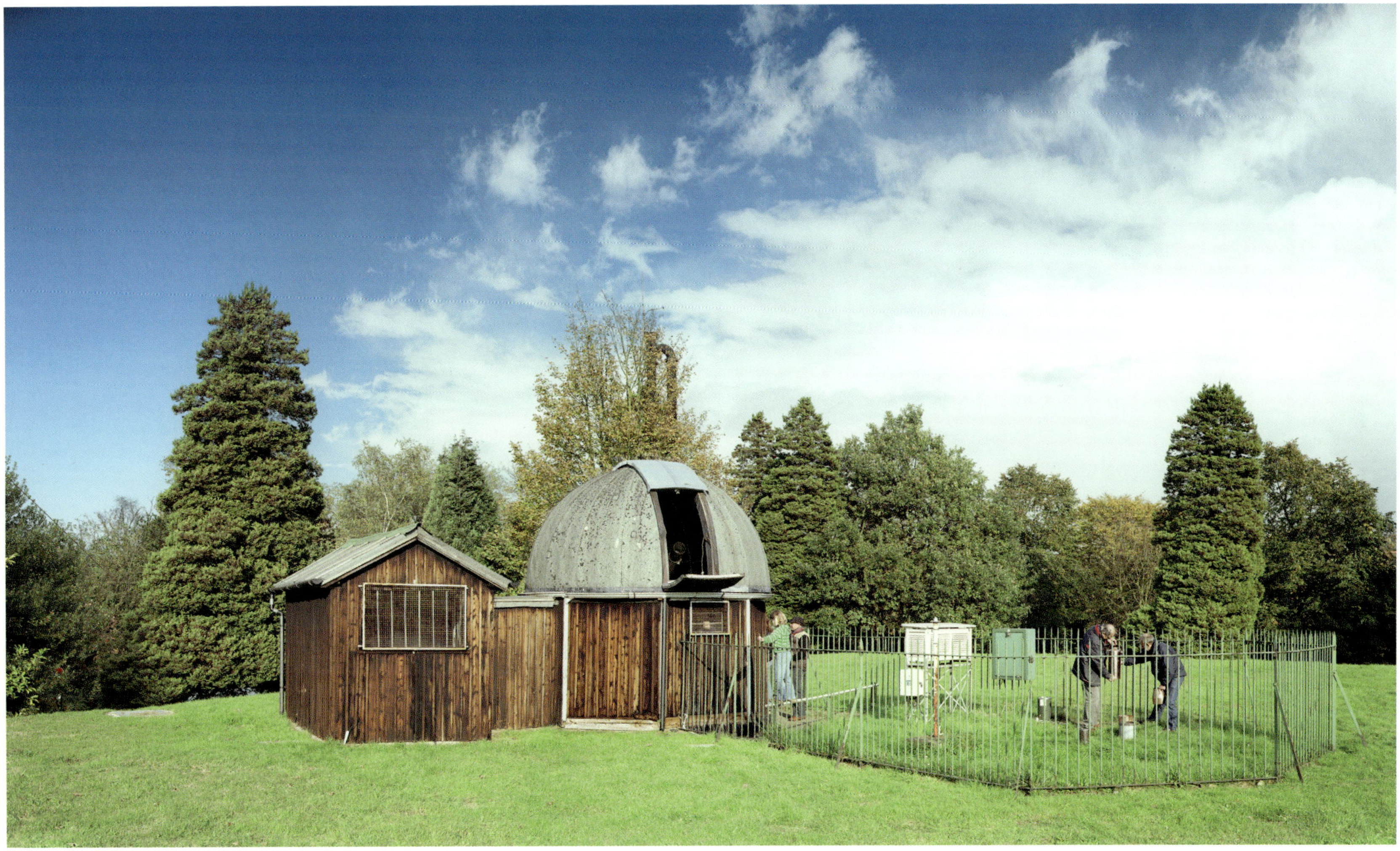

**23** Hampstead Reservoir Observatory at Lower Terrace, near Whitestone Pond (edition 3/5) 2006

**23** Hampstead Observatory au sommet du réservoir à Lower Terrace, près de Whitestone Pond (édition 3/5) 2006

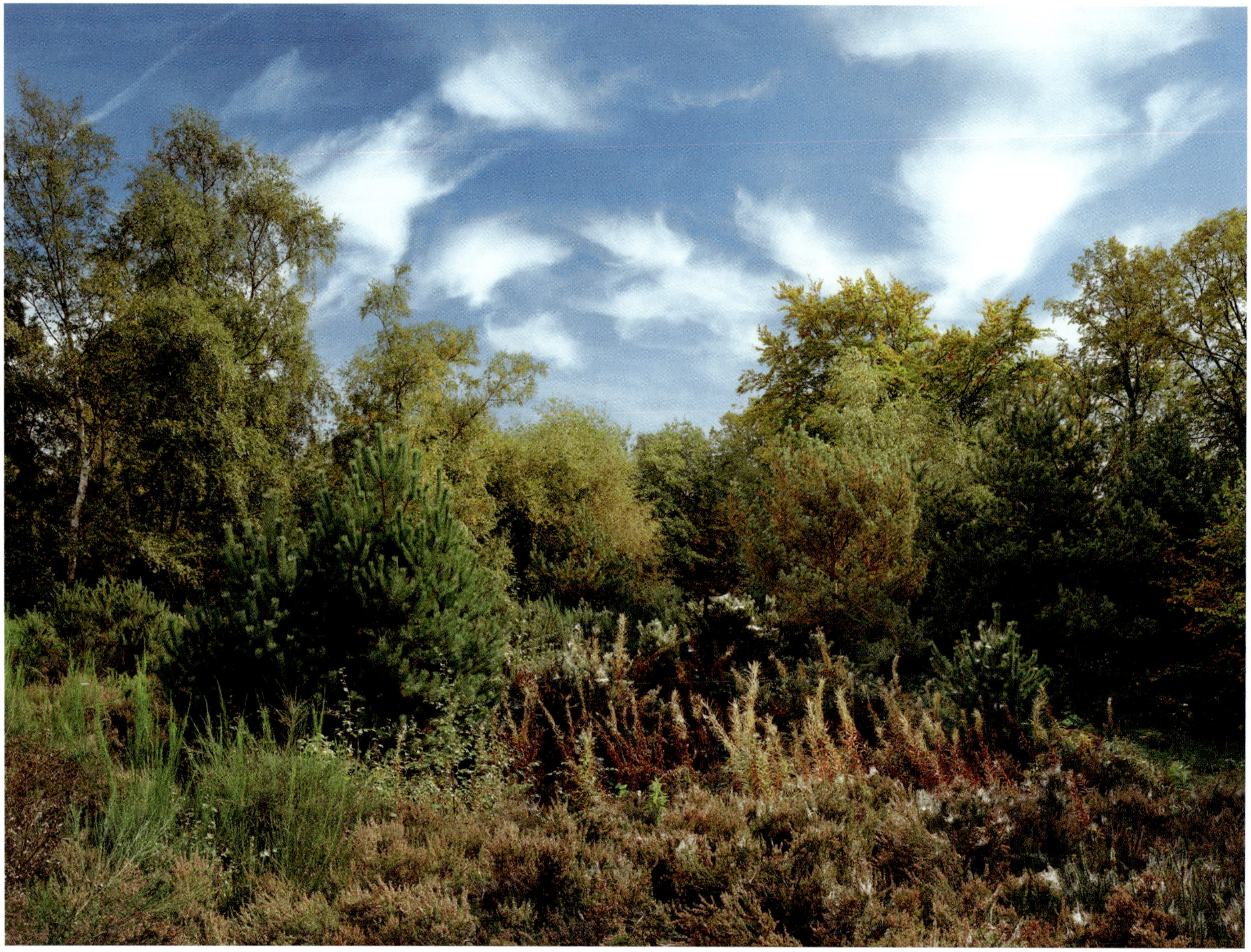

**24** Trees and Sky, West Heath (edition 2/5) 2008

**24** Arbres et ciel, West Heath (édition 2/5) 2008

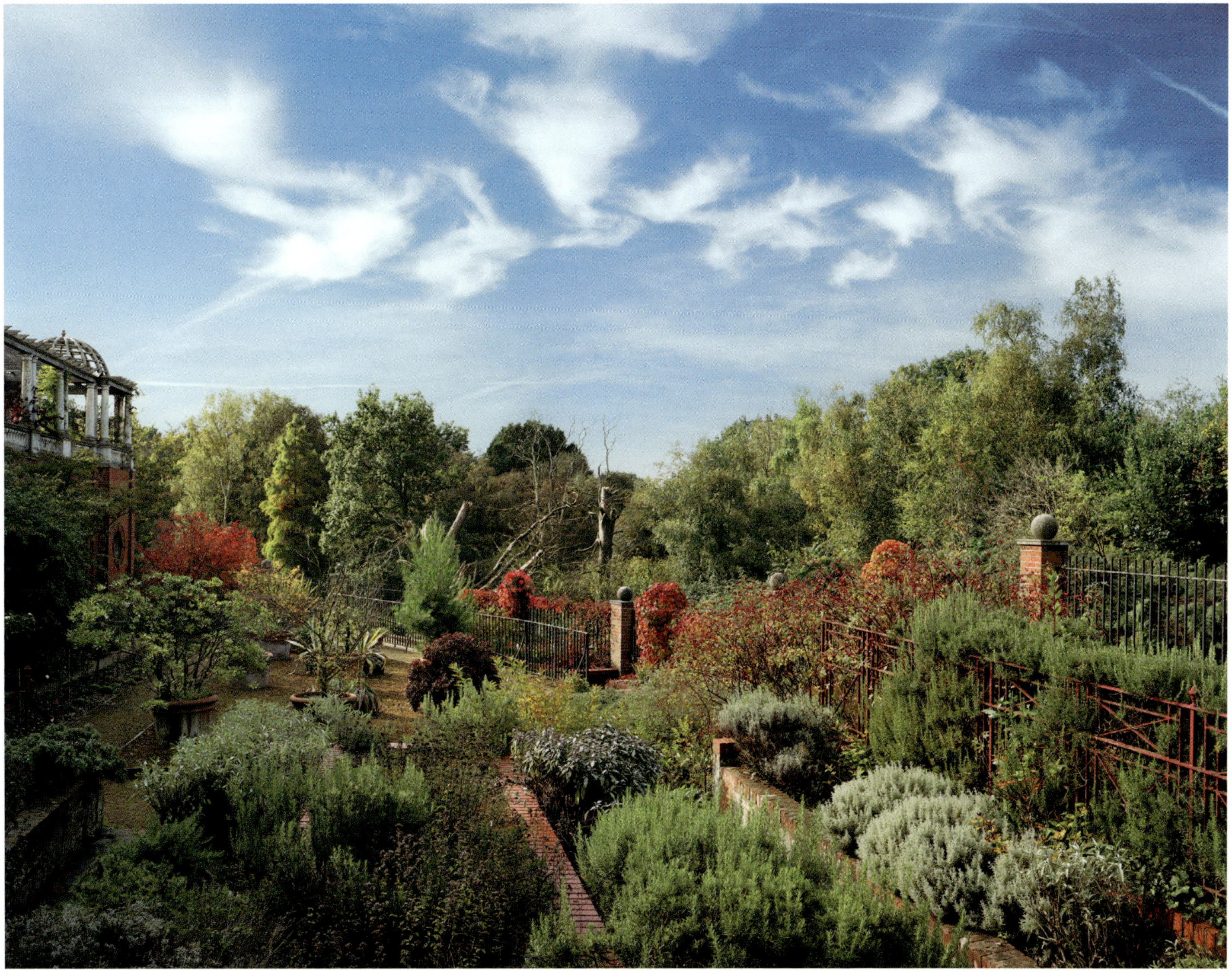

**25** Hill Garden Pergola at Inverforth House (edition 3/5)
2007

**25** Pergola de Hill Garden, Inverforth House (édition 3/5)
2007

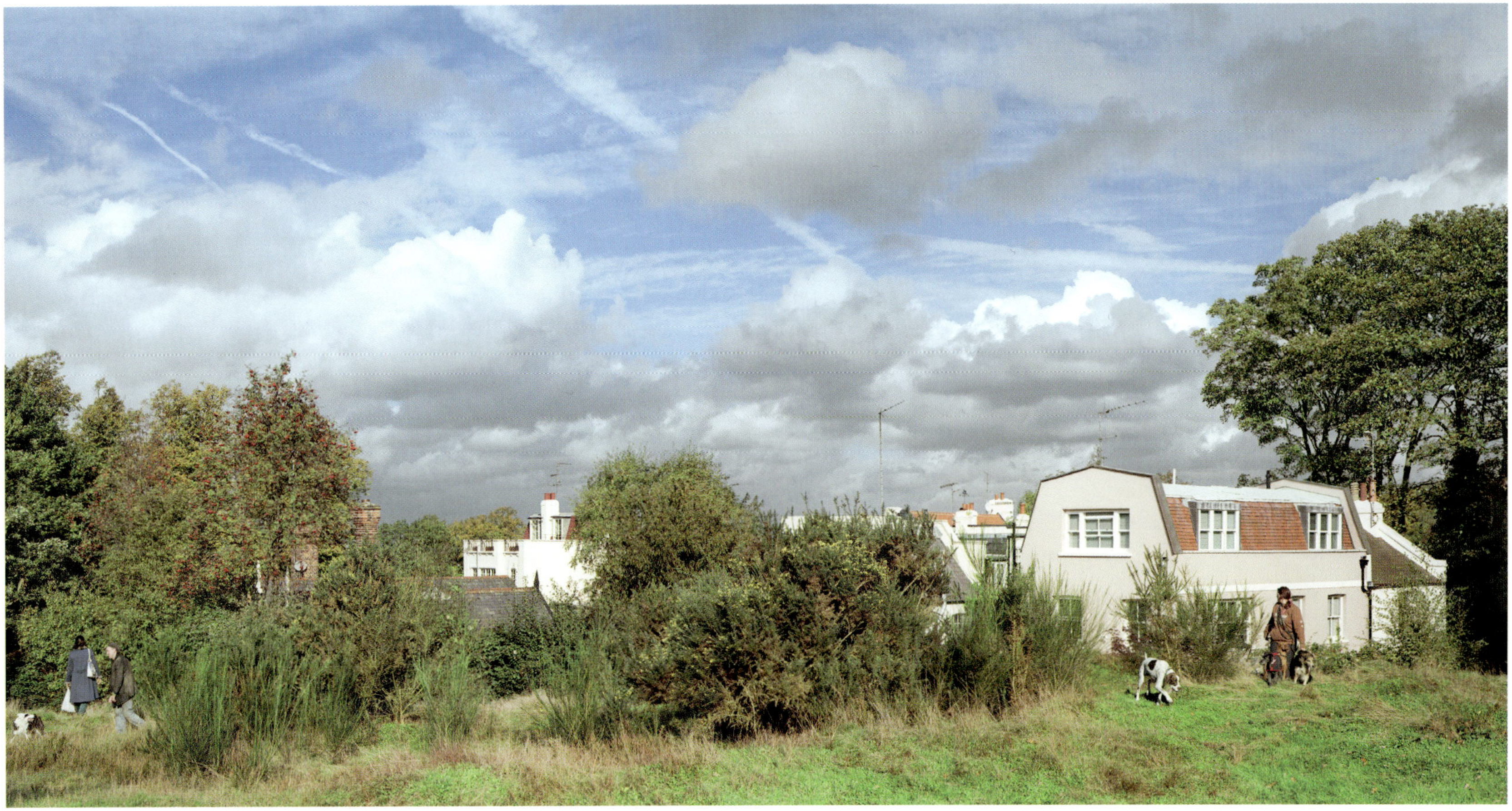

**26** View of Rooke House, Looking Towards Highgate (edition 1/5) 2006

**26** Vue de Rooke House, vers Highgate (édition 1/5) 2006

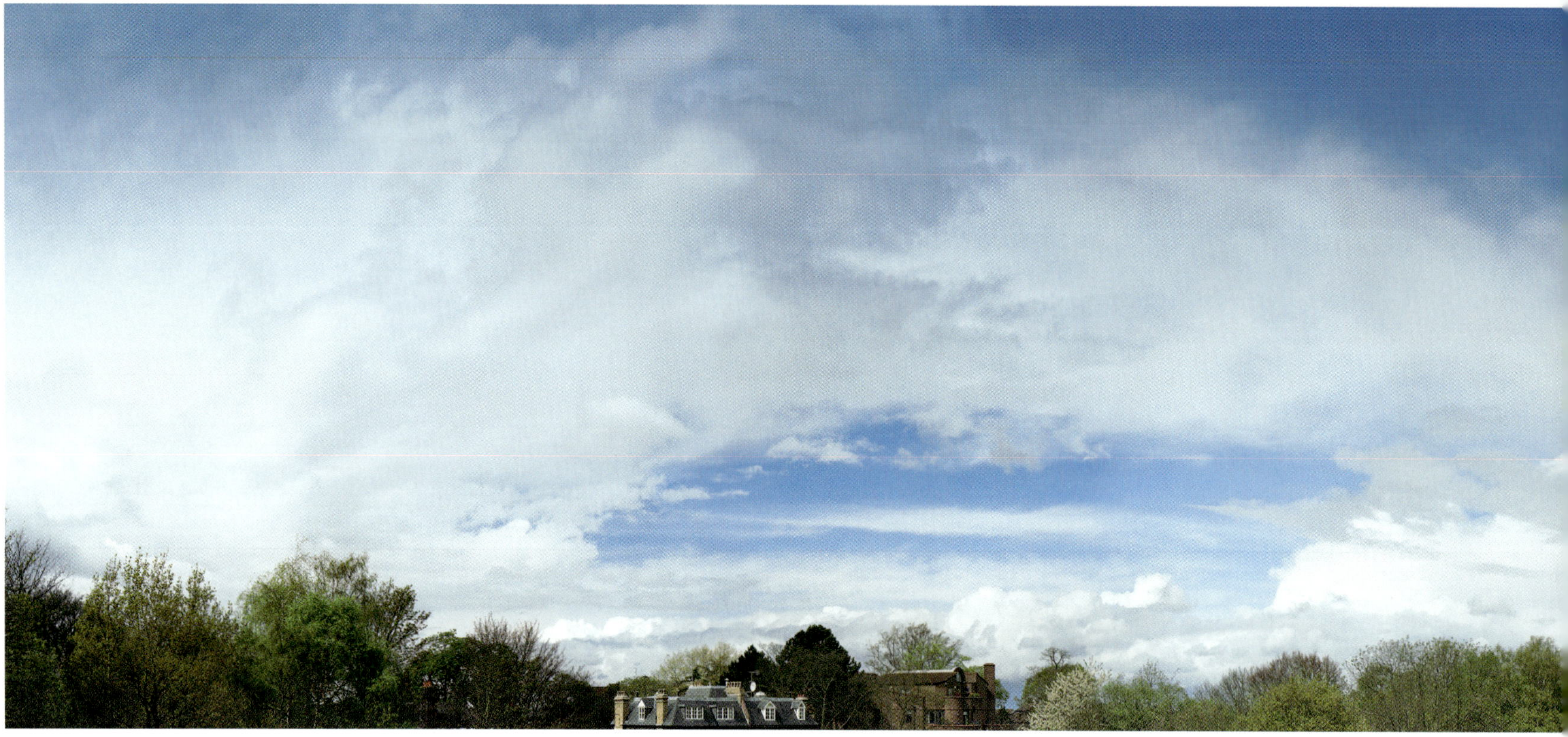

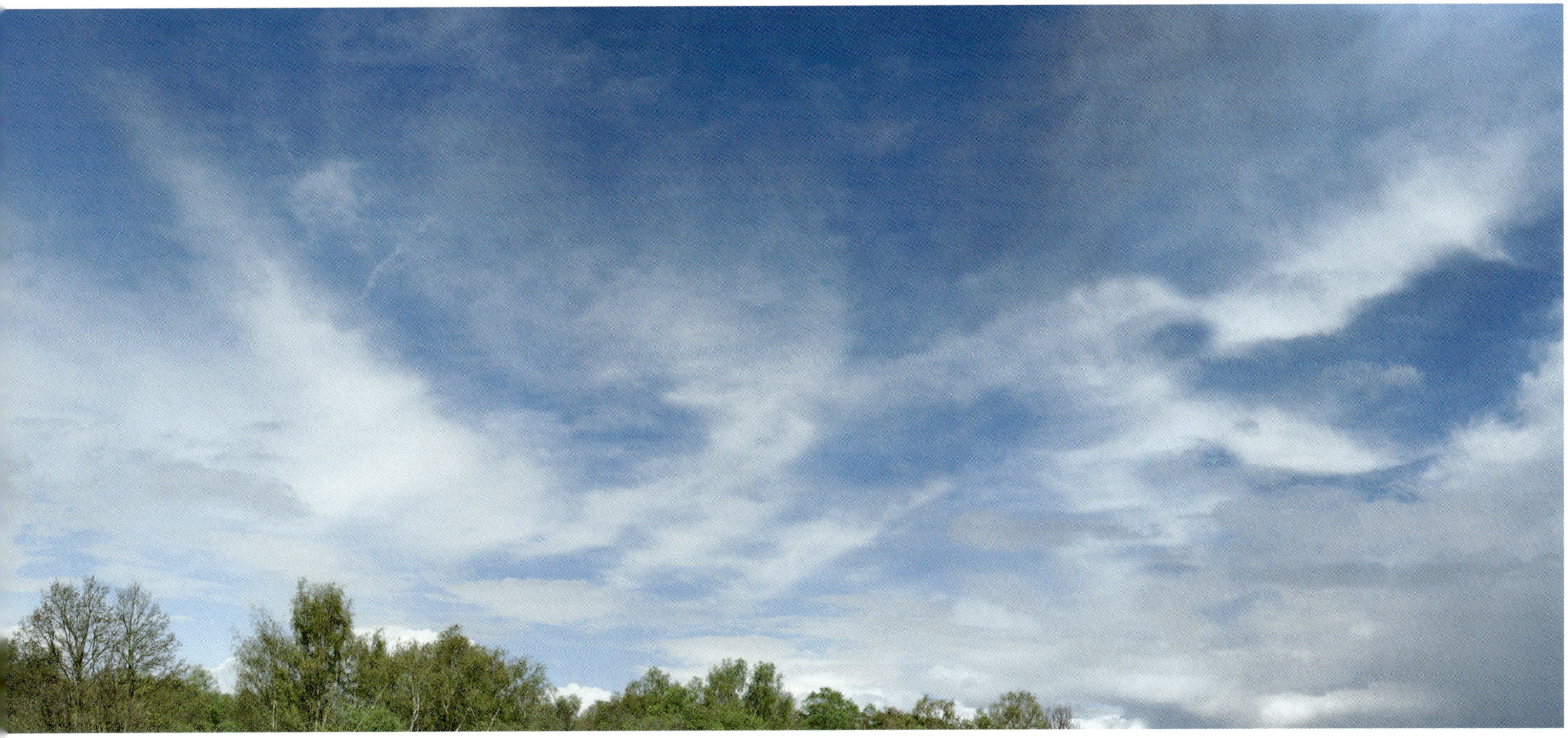

**27** Judges Walk, Looking Towards Jack Straw Castle (edition 1/5) 2008

**27** Judges Walk, vers Jack Straw Castle (édition 1/5) 2008

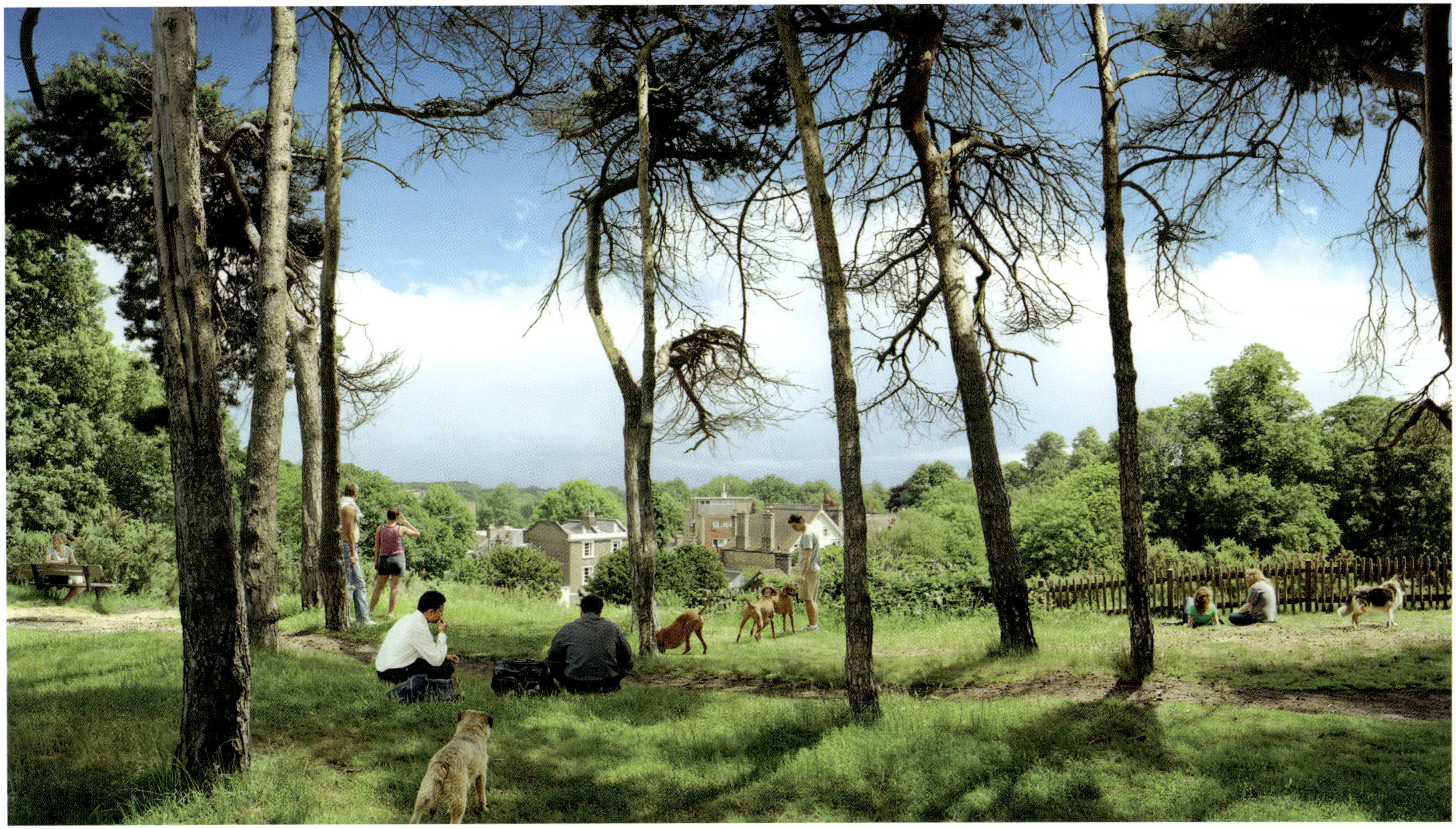

**28** View of Vale of Health, Looking Towards Hampstead (edition 5/5) 2007

**28** Vue de Vale of Health, vers Hampstead (édition 5/5) 2007

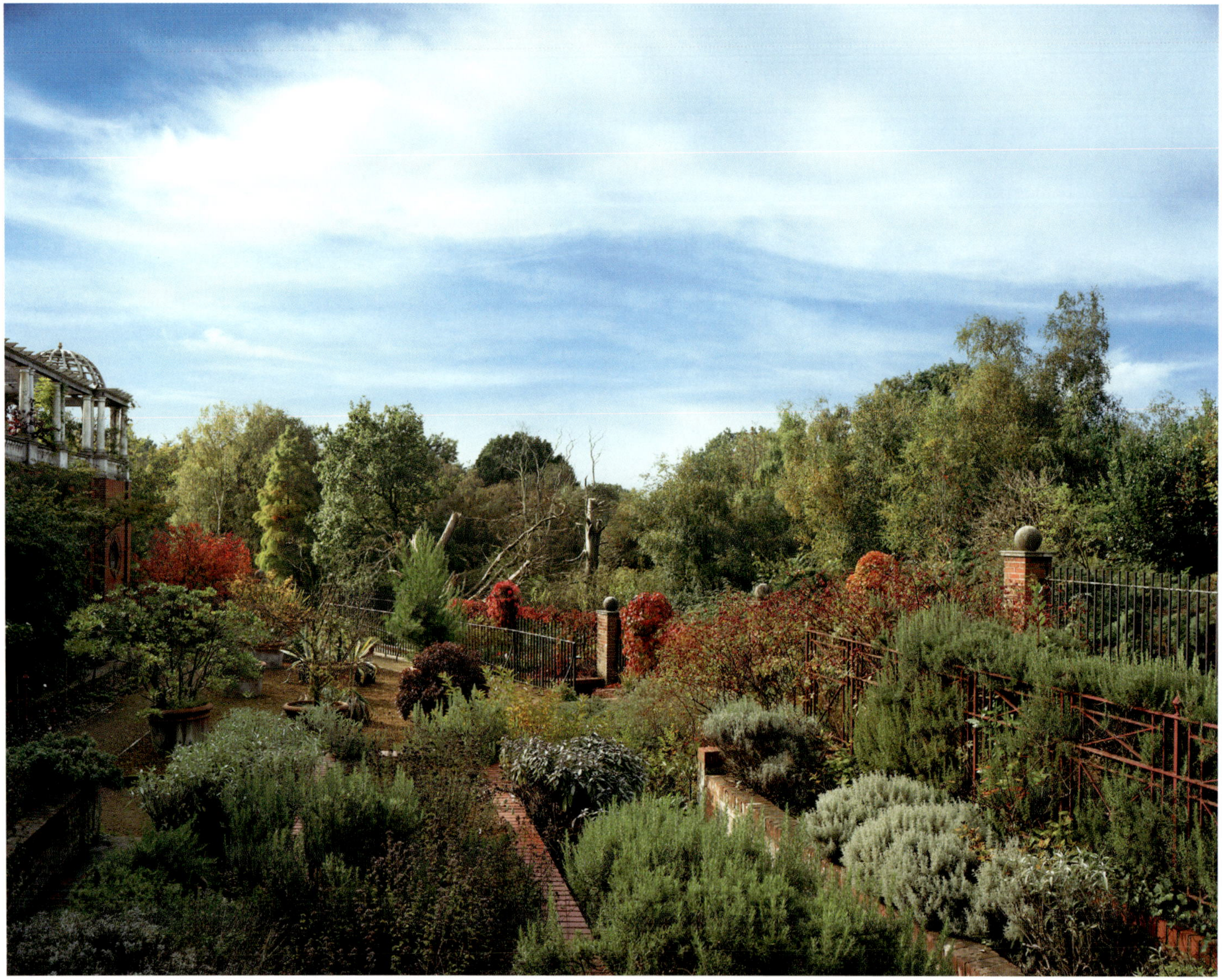

**29** Hill Garden Pergola at Inverforth House (edition 2/5)
2007

**29** Pergola de Hill Garden, Inverforth House (édition 2/5)
2007

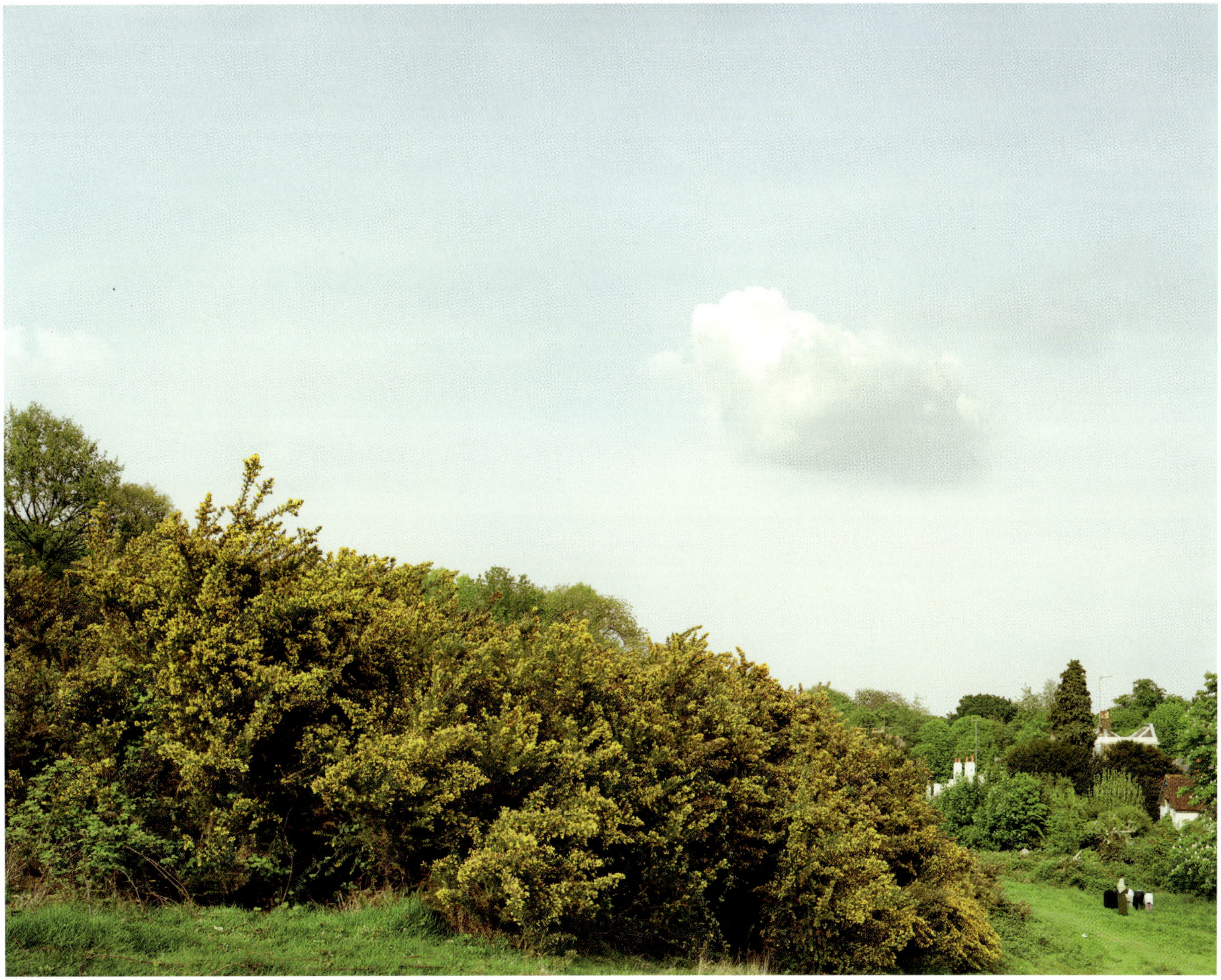

**30** Gorse and Sky (edition 4/5) 2008

**30** Ajonc et ciel (édition 4/5) 2008

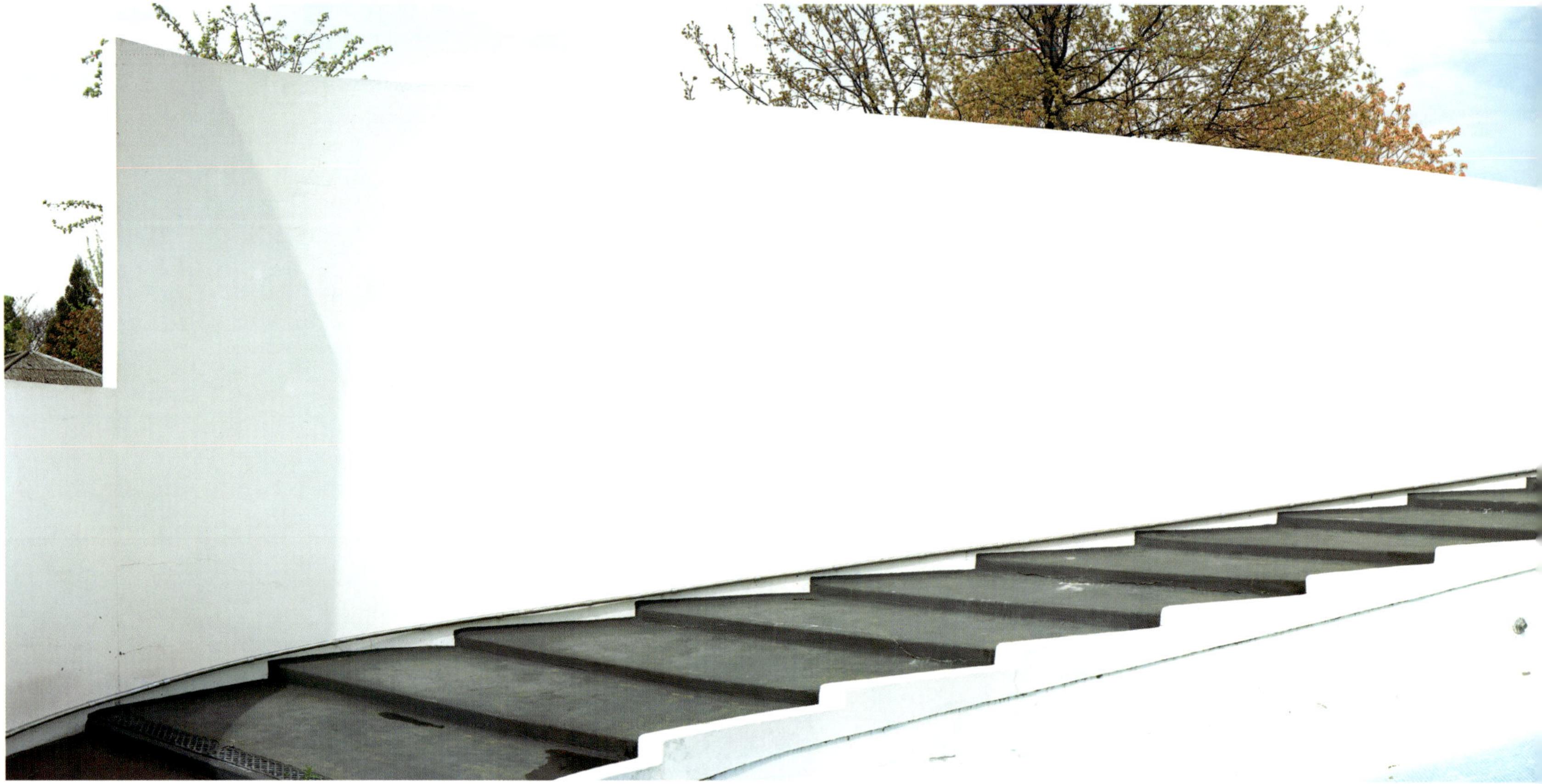

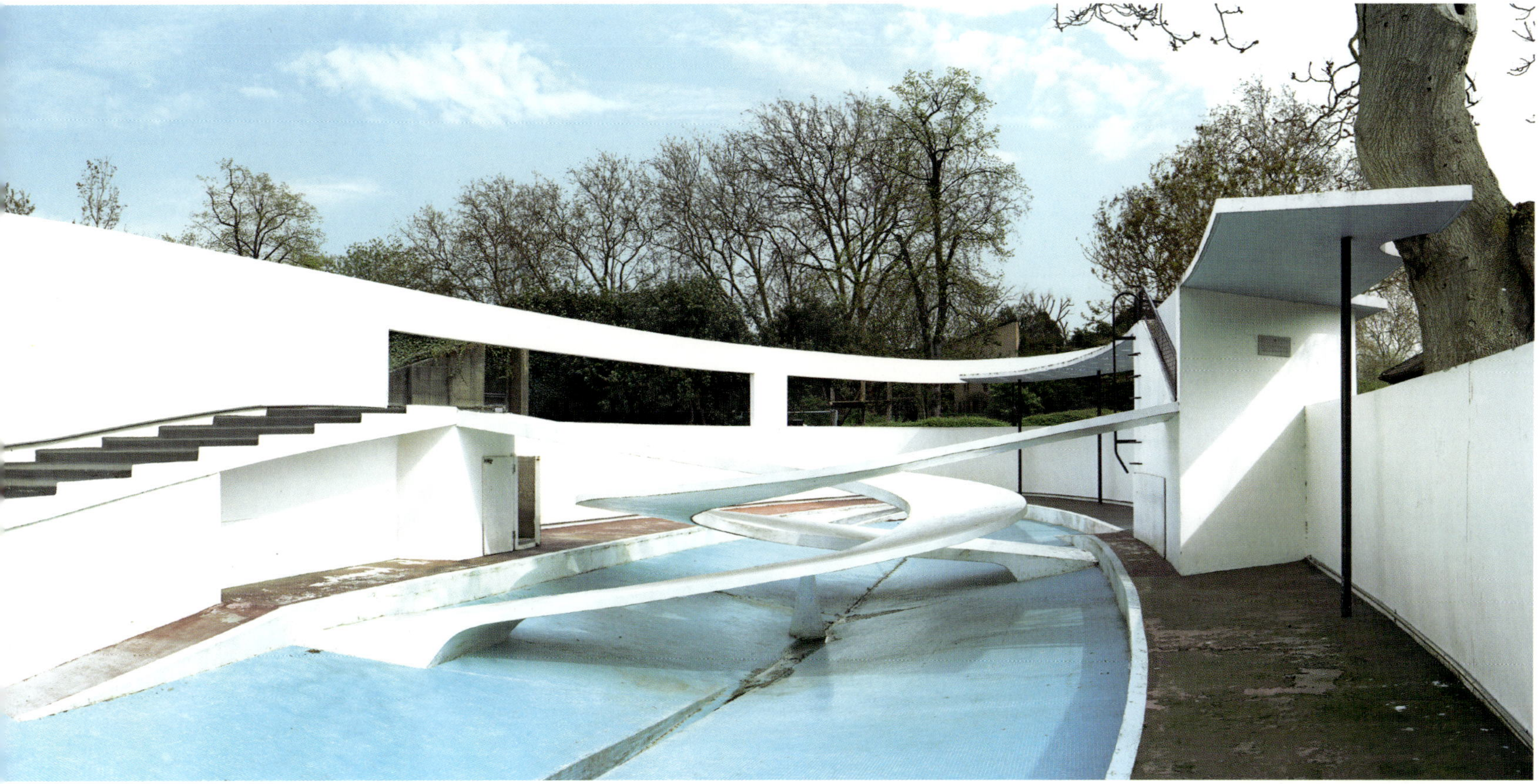

**31** Emptied Penguin Pool, London Zoo, May 2008, Architect: Berthold Lubetkin, 1934 2008

**31** Piscine de manchots vide, London Zoo, mai 2008, architecte : Berthold Lubetkin, 1934 2008

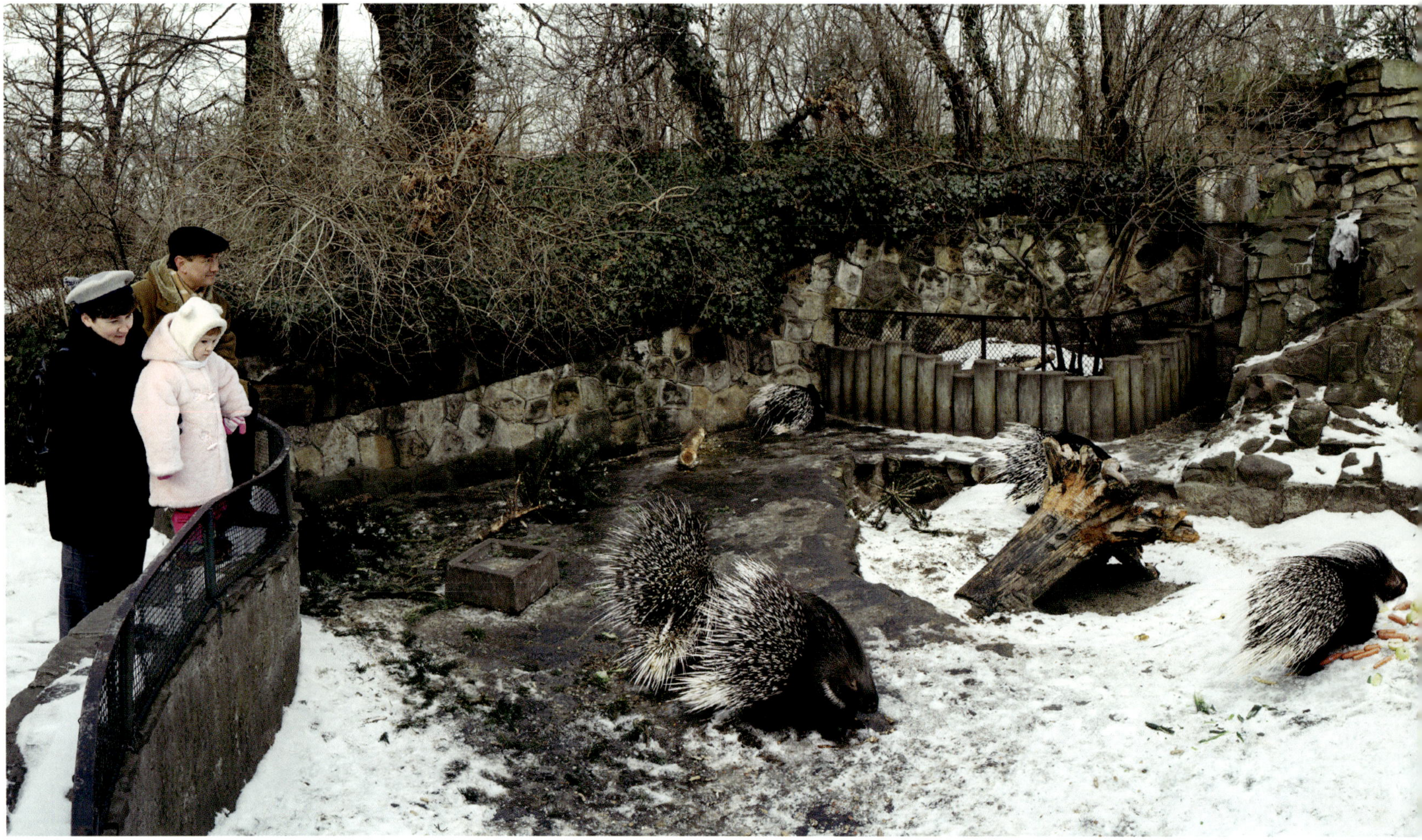

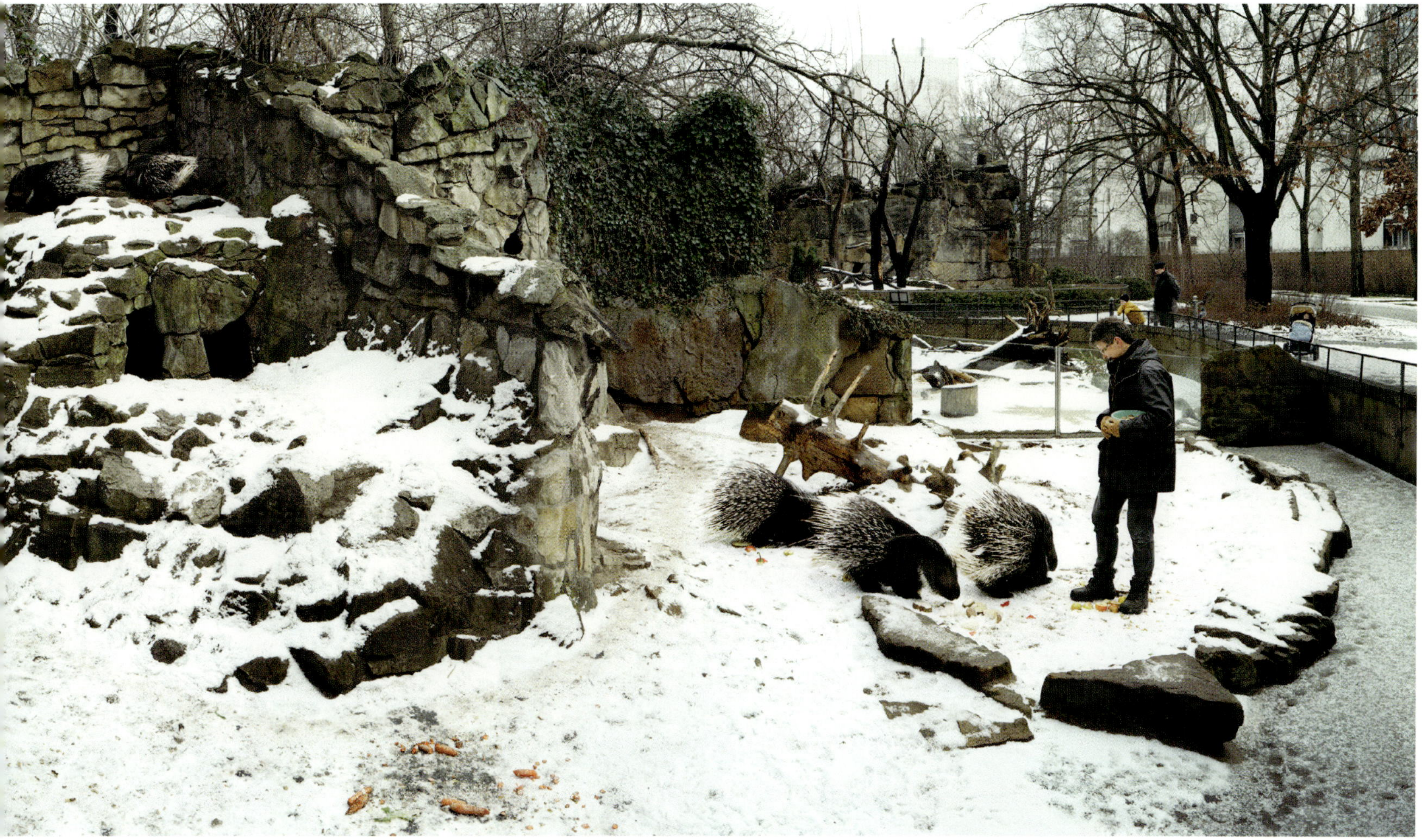

**32** Display for Porcupines (Hystrix africae australis), Zoologischer Garten, Berlin 2006

**32** Enclos des porcs-épics (Hystrix africae australis), Zoologischer Garten, Berlin 2006

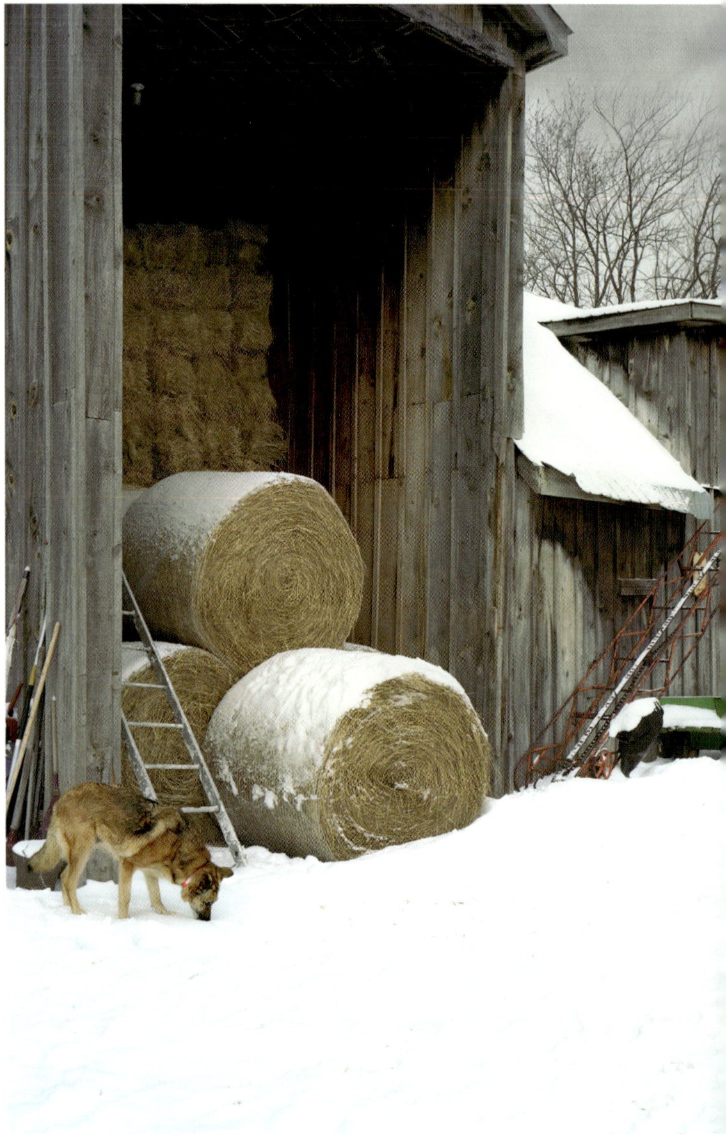

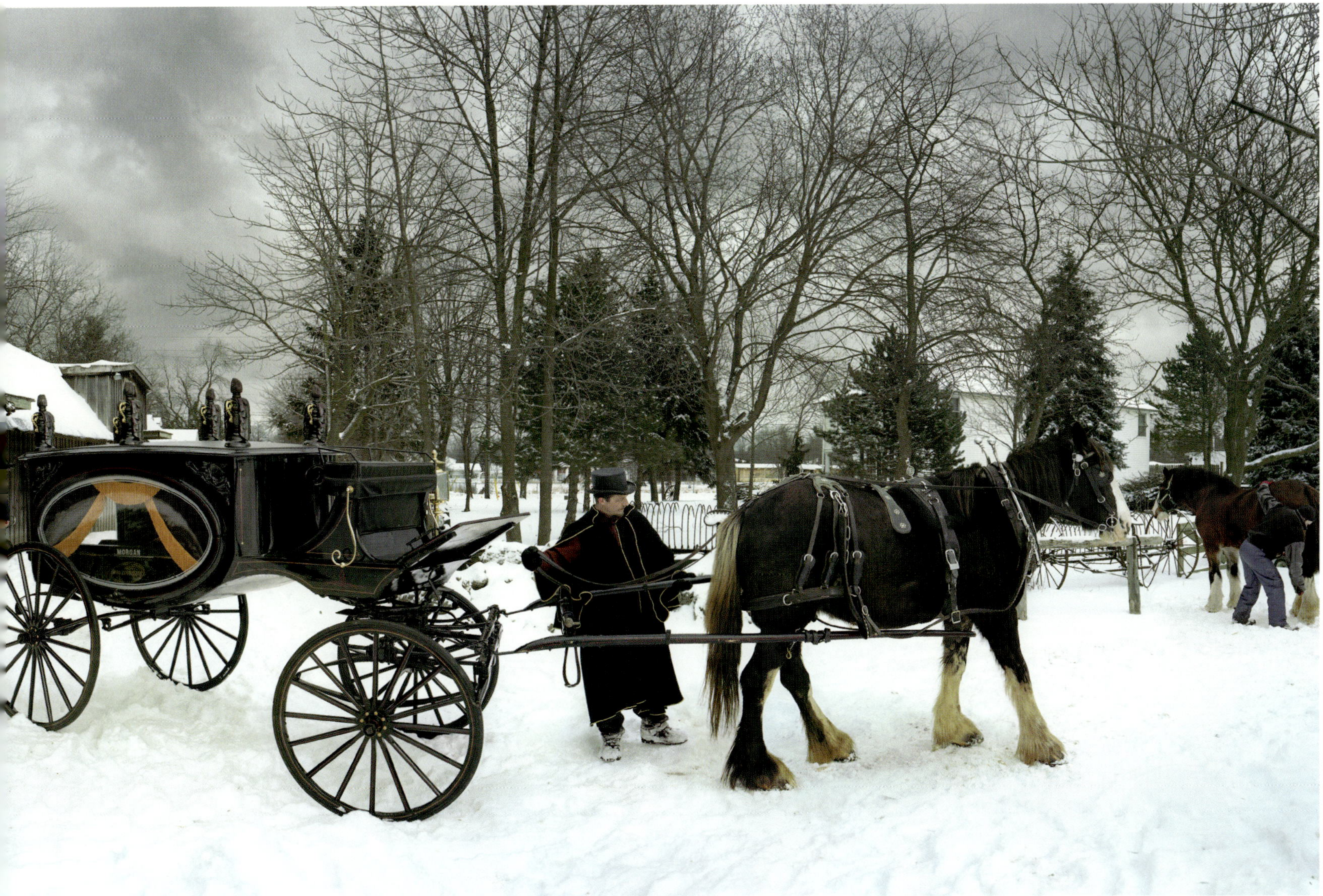

**33** A Horse Drawn Hearse, Queens Royal Tours, 174 Anne, Niagara-on-the-Lake, Ontario 2009

**33** Un corbillard hippomobile, Queens Royal Tours, 174, Anne, Niagara-on-the-Lake, Ontario 2009

# Biography

Scott McFarland was born in Hamilton, Ontario, in 1975, and grew up in Fort McMurray and Calgary, Alberta. In 1997, he received his BFA from the University of British Columbia, Vancouver. He presently lives and works in Vancouver and Toronto.

## Exhibitions and Publications

**1998**

*Scott McFarland*, Or Gallery, Vancouver
*Edge City*, Surrey Art Gallery, Surrey, BC

Chris Brayshaw, *Edge City* (Surrey: Surrey Art Gallery).

**1999**

*After Photography*, Monte Clark Gallery, Vancouver

Roy Arden, *After Photography* (Vancouver: Monte Clark Gallery).
Blake Gopnik, "Reticence in Photography is Good, Interview with Jeff Wall," *The Globe and Mail*, 6 November.



**2000**

Roy Arden, "After Photography," *Canadian Art*, vol. 14, no. 4 (winter), pp. 48–56.
"Artist's Project," *Adbusters*, no. 29. The Media Foundation.

**2001**

*These Days*, Vancouver Art Gallery, Vancouver

Chris Brayshaw, "Garden Optics," *CV Photo*, no. 54, pp. 7–13.

**2002**

*Imago*, Salamanca, Spain

*Imago 2002* (Salamanca: Salamanca New Art Centre).

**2003**

*Boathouse*, Monte Clark Gallery, Toronto
*Coastal Cabin*, Contemporary Art Gallery, Vancouver

William Wood, Reid Shier and Owen Kydd, *Scott McFarland: Cabin Photographs* (Vancouver: Contemporary Art Gallery).

**2004**

*Everything Gone Green, Photography and the Garden*, National Museum of Photography, Film and Television (National Media Museum), Bradford, UK
*Fabulation*, VOX, Montreal

Sarah Thorton, "Nocturnes," *Contemporary*, no. 62, pp. 32–37.
"Scott McFarland: A Photographer in the Garden (Artist's Project)," *Canadian Art*, vol. 21, no. 2 (summer), pp. 58–62.

**2005**

*Scott McFarland: Analyzing – Trapping – Inspecting*, Union Gallery, London, UK
*Another Photography*, Regen Projects, Los Angeles
*Intertidal: Vancouver Art & Artists*, MuHKA, Antwerp, Belgium
*Real Pictures: Photographs from the Collection of Claudia Beck and Andrew Gruft*, Vancouver Art Gallery, Vancouver
*The Space of Making*, Neuer Berliner Kunstverein, Berlin, Germany. Touring to Kunstmuseum Heidenheim, Kunstsammlungen der Städtische Museen Zwickau, Städtische Galerie Waldkraiburg, Germany
*Variations on the Picturesque*, Kitchener-Waterloo Art Gallery, Kitchener

*Intertidal: Vancouver Art & Artists* (Antwerp: MuHKA).
"Scott McFarland: Empire (Artist's Project)," in Robert Bean, ed., *Image and Inscription, an Anthology of Contemporary Canadian Photography* (Toronto: YYZ Books), pp. 131–137.
Marie-Josée Jean, *The Space of Making. Contemporary Photographic Art from Canada* (Berlin: Neuer Berliner Kunstverein).
Sarah Harrison, "Scott McFarland," *ArtReview*, April, p. 105.
Lee Henderson, "The Empire Grows Back," *Border Crossings*, no. 94 (summer), pp. 50–56.
David Pagel, "Moments Captured – and Combined," *Los Angeles Times*, 21 October, p. 27.

**2006**

*A History of Photography*, Victoria and Albert Museum, London, UK
*Boys and Flowers*, Western Bridge, Seattle
*Clickdoubleclick*, Haus der Kunst, Munich, Germany
*Grid < > Matrix*, Mildred Lane Kemper Art Museum, St Louis
*Landscape: Recent Acquisitions*, The Museum of Modern Art, New York

Jean-Francois Chevrier, *Click Doubleclick: The Documentary Factor*, Thomas Weski, ed. (Cologne: Walther König, Haus der Kunst), pp. 270–275, 312.

## Biographie

Scott McFarland naît en 1975 à Hamilton, en Ontario, et grandit à Fort McMurray et à Calgary, en Alberta. En 1997, il obtient un baccalauréat en beaux-arts de l'University of British Columbia, à Vancouver. Il vit et travaille actuellement à Vancouver et Toronto.

### Expositions et publications

**1998**

*Scott McFarland*, Or Gallery, Vancouver
*Edge City*, Surrey Art Gallery, Surrey, C.-B.

Chris Brayshaw, *Edge City*, Surrey, Surrey Art Gallery.

**1999**

*After Photography*, Monte Clark Gallery, Vancouver

Roy Arden, *After Photography*, Vancouver, Monte Clark Gallery.
Blake Gopnik, « Reticence in Photography is Good, Interview with Jeff Wall », *The Globe and Mail*, 6 novembre.

**2000**

Roy Arden, « After Photography », *Canadian Art*, vol. 14, n° 4 (hiver), p. 48–56.
« Artist's Project », *Adbusters*, n° 29, The Media Foundation.

**2001**

*These Days*, Musée des beaux-arts de Vancouver, Vancouver

Chris Brayshaw, « Garden Optics », *CV Photo*, n° 54, p. 7–13.

**2002**

*Imago*, Salamanque, Espagne

*Imago 2002*, Salamanque, Salamanca New Art Centre.

**2003**

*Boathouse*, Monte Clark Gallery, Toronto
*Coastal Cabin*, Contemporary Art Gallery, Vancouver

William Wood, Reid Shier et Owen Kydd, *Scott McFarland: Cabin Photographs*, Vancouver, Contemporary Art Gallery.

**2004**

*Everything Gone Green, Photography and the Garden*, National Museum of Photography, Film and Television (National Media Museum), Bradford, R.-U.
*Fabulation*, VOX, Montréal

Sarah Thorton, « Nocturnes », *Contemporary*, n° 62, p. 32–37.
« Scott McFarland: A Photographer in the Garden (Artist's Project) », *Canadian Art*, vol. 21, n° 2 (été), p. 58–62.

**2005**

*Scott McFarland: Analyzing – Trapping – Inspecting*, Union Gallery, Londres, R.-U.
*Another Photography*, Regen Projects, Los Angeles
*Intertidal: Vancouver Art & Artists*, MuHKA, Anvers, Belgique
*Real Pictures: Photographs from the Collection of Claudia Beck and Andrew Gruft*, Musée des beaux-arts de Vancouver, Vancouver
*The Space of Making*, Neuer Berliner Kunstverein, Berlin, Allemagne. En tournée aux Kunstmuseum Heidenheim, Kunstsammlungen der Städtische Museen Zwickau, Städtische Galerie Waldkraiburg, Allemagne
*Variations on the Picturesque*, Kitchener-Waterloo Art Gallery, Kitchener

*Intertidal: Vancouver Art & Artists*, Anvers, MuHKA.
« Scott McFarland: Empire (Artist's Project) », dans Robert Bean (sous la direction de), *Image and Inscription, an Anthology of Contemporary Canadian Photography*, Toronto, YYZ Books, p. 131–137.
Marie-Josée Jean, *The Space of Making. Contemporary Photographic Art from Canada*, Berlin, Neuer Berliner Kunstverein.
Sarah Harrison, « Scott McFarland », *ArtReview*, avril, p. 105.
Lee Henderson, « The Empire Grows Back », *Border Crossings*, n° 94 (été), p. 50–56.
David Pagel, « Moments Captured – and Combined », *Los Angeles Times*, 21 octobre, p. 27.

**2006**

*A History of Photography*, Victoria and Albert Museum, Londres, R.-U.
*Boys and Flowers*, Western Bridge, Seattle
*Clickdoubleclick*, Haus der Kunst, Munich, Allemagne
*Grid < > Matrix*, Mildred Lane Kemper Art Museum, St Louis
*Landscape: Recent Acquisitions*, The Museum of Modern Art, New York

**2006 (continued)**
Vincent Honoré, "Scott McFarland," in T.J. Demos and Editors of Phaidon Books, *Vitamin Ph: New Perspectives in Photography* (London: Phaidon Press Limited), pp. 182–185, 343.
Adam Harrison, "Scott McFarland," *Canadian Art*, spring, pp. 86–87.

**2007**
*Acting the Part: Photography as Theatre*, Vancouver Art Gallery, Vancouver
*Crack the Sky, Biennale de Montréal 2007*, Montreal
*Garden of Eden*, Kunsthalle, Emden, Germany
*New Photography 2007*, The Museum of Modern Art, New York
*Re-Envisioning Habitat*, Oakville Galleries, Oakville
*Sound and Vision*, Centre culturel canadien, Paris, France

Chris Balaschak, "Scott McFarland," *Frieze*, October, p. 293.

**2009**
*Scott McFarland*, Vancouver Art Gallery, Vancouver

**Collections**

Albright-Knox Art Gallery, Buffalo
Art Gallery of Ontario, Toronto
Canadian Museum of Contemporary Photography, Ottawa
Centro de Arte de Salamanca, Spain
Glenbow Museum, Calgary
Justina M. Barnicke Gallery, Hart House, University of Toronto, Toronto
K21, Dusseldorf, Germany
Mendel Art Gallery, Saskatoon
Morris and Helen Belkin Art Gallery, University of British Columbia, Vancouver
National Gallery of Canada, Ottawa
National Media Museum, Bradford, UK
Oakville Galleries, Oakville
San Francisco Museum of Modern Art, San Francisco
The Montreal Museum of Fine Arts, Montreal
The Museum of Modern Art, New York
Vancouver Art Gallery, Vancouver
Victoria and Albert Museum, London, UK
Walker Art Center, Minneapolis

**2006 (suite)**

Jean-François Chevrier, *Click Doubleclick: The Documentary Factor*, Thomas Weski (sous la direction de), Cologne, Walther König, Haus der Kunst, p. 270–275, 312.

Vincent Honoré, « Scott McFarland », dans T.J. Demos et Editors of Phaidon Books, *Vitamin Ph: New Perspectives in Photography*, Londres, Phaidon Press Limited, p. 182–185, 343; version française, Rodrigo Alonso, Thomas Boutoux, Isolde Brielmaier, et coll., *Vitamine Ph : nouvelles perspectives en photographie*, trad. par Laure Bataillou, Hélène Ladjadj et Elisabeth Luc, Paris, Phaidon, 2007.

Adam Harrison, « Scott McFarland », *Canadian Art*, printemps, p. 86–87.

**2007**

*Acting the Part: Photography as Theatre*, Musée des beaux-arts de Vancouver, Vancouver

*Remuer ciel et terre, Biennale de Montréal 2007*, Montréal

*Garden of Eden*, Kunsthalle, Emden, Allemagne

*New Photography 2007*, The Museum of Modern Art, New York

*Re-Envisioning Habitat*, Oakville Galleries, Oakville

*Son et vision*, Centre culturel canadien, Paris, France

Chris Balaschak, « Scott McFarland », *Frieze*, octobre, p. 293.

**2009**

*Scott McFarland*, Musée des beaux-arts de Vancouver, Vancouver

## Collections

Albright-Knox Art Gallery, Buffalo
Centro de Arte de Salamanca, Espagne
Musée Glenbow, Calgary
Justina M. Barnicke Gallery, Hart House, University of Toronto, Toronto
K21, Düsseldorf, Allemagne
Mendel Art Gallery, Saskatoon
Morris and Helen Belkin Art Gallery, University of British Columbia, Vancouver
Musée canadien de la photographie contemporaine, Ottawa
Musée des beaux-arts de Montréal, Montréal
Musée des beaux-arts de l'Ontario, Toronto
Musée des beaux-arts de Vancouver, Vancouver
Musée des beaux-arts du Canada, Ottawa
National Media Museum, Bradford, R.-U.
Oakville Galleries, Oakville
San Francisco Museum of Modern Art, San Francisco
The Museum of Modern Art, New York
Victoria and Albert Museum, Londres, R.-U.
Walker Art Center, Minneapolis

## List of Works

Dimensions are height × width.

*Filtering, Peter Harrison Changing Water Pump Filter*
2002 (not illustrated)
From the series *Gardens*
Dye coupler print
102 × 122 cm
National Gallery of Canada, Ottawa
41186

*Pouring, Ben Kubomiwa Treating Fountain with Potassium Permanganate* 2002 (plate 1)
From the series *Gardens*
Dye coupler print
102 × 122 cm
National Gallery of Canada, Ottawa
41185

*Analyzing, Ryan Otto Conducts Water Test* 2003 (figure 2, detail)
From the series *Gardens*
Chromogenic print
102 × 122 cm
Collection of Christopher Wood



*Inspecting, Allan O'Connor Searches for Botrytis cinerea* 2003 (figure 1, detail, plate 5)
From the series *Gardens*
Chromogenic print
102 × 122 cm
Courtesy of the Artist and Union Gallery, London, UK

*Trapping, Ernesto Gacutan Positions Against Fauna* 2003 (plate 6)
From the series *Gardens*
Chromogenic print
102 × 122 cm
Courtesy of the Artist and Union Gallery, London, UK

*Dipping, Conrad Arida with Mother and Child Wading in the Water* 2004 (plate 9)
From the series *Gardens*
Chromogenic print
102 × 122 cm
Private Collection, Toronto

*Fountain Study, Late Fall; Cedrus atlantica, Acer palmatum, Populus nigra* 2004 (plate 2)
From the series *Gardens*
Chromogenic print
102 × 279 cm
Collection of the Families of Steven Latner and Michael Latner

*On the Terrace Garden, Joe and Rosalee Segal with Cosmos atrosanguineus* 2004 (plate 7)
From the series *Gardens*
Chromogenic print
102 × 122 cm
Courtesy of the Artist and Union Gallery, London, UK

*Orchard View, Late Spring; Vitis vinifera, Wisteria* 2004 (plate 3)
From the series *Gardens*
Chromogenic print
102 × 305 cm
Canadian Museum of Contemporary Photography, Ottawa
2005.91

*Spraying, Norman Whaley Applying Aphid Solution* 2004 (plate 4)
From the series *Gardens*
Chromogenic print
102 × 122 cm
Courtesy of the Artist and Union Gallery, London, UK

*Discussing, Michael O'Brian with Artist and Model on his Property* 2005 (plate 8)
From the series *Gardens*
Chromogenic print
102 × 122 cm
RBC Royal Bank

*Orchard on Dr. Young's Property, 3226 W. 51st. Vancouver* 2005 (plate 10)
From the series *Gardens*
Ink jet print
102 × 305 cm
William J. Hokin Collection

*Stables on Dr. Young's Property, 3226 W. 51st. Vancouver* 2005 (plate 11)
From the series *Gardens*
Ink jet print
102 × 305 cm
William J. Hokin Collection

## Liste des œuvres

Les dimensions des œuvres sont données dans l'ordre suivant : hauteur, largeur.

*Filtrer, Peter Harrison change le filtre d'une pompe à eau* 2002 (non reproduite)
De la série *Jardins*
Épreuve à développement chromogène
102 × 122 cm
Musée des beaux-arts du Canada, Ottawa
41186

*Verser, Ben Kubomiwa traite la fontaine avec du permanganate de potassium* 2002 (planche 1)
De la série *Jardins*
Épreuve à développement chromogène
102 × 122 cm
Musée des beaux-arts du Canada, Ottawa
41185

*Analyser, Ryan Otto teste l'eau* 2003 (figure 2, détail)
De la série *Jardins*
Épreuve à développement chromogène
102 × 122 cm
Collection de Christopher Wood

*Inspecter, Allan O'Connor cherche du Botrytis cinerea* 2003 (figure 1, détail, planche 5)
De la série *Jardins*
Épreuve à développement chromogène
102 × 122 cm
Avec l'aimable autorisation de l'artiste et de l'Union Gallery, Londres, R.-U.

*Piéger, Ernesto Gacutan met en place un piège contre la faune* 2003 (planche 6)
De la série *Jardins*
Épreuve à développement chromogène
102 × 122 cm
Avec l'aimable autorisation de l'artiste et de l'Union Gallery, Londres, R.-U.

*Baigner, Conrad Arida avec mère et enfant pataugeant dans l'eau* 2004 (planche 9)
De la série *Jardins*
Épreuve à développement chromogène
102 × 122 cm
Collection particulière, Toronto

*Étude d'une fontaine, à la fin de l'automne. Cedrus atlantica, Acer palmatum, Populus nigra* 2004 (planche 2)
De la série *Jardins*
Épreuve à développement chromogène
102 × 279 cm
Collection des familles de Steven Latner et Michael Latner

*Dans le jardin de la terrasse, Joe et Rosalee Segal avec du Cosmos atrosanguineus* 2004 (planche 7)
De la série *Jardins*
Épreuve à développement chromogène
102 × 122 cm
Avec l'aimable autorisation de l'artiste et de l'Union Gallery, Londres, R.-U.

*Vue d'un verger, à la fin du printemps. Vitis vinifera, Wisteria* 2004 (planche 3)
De la série *Jardins*
Épreuve à développement chromogène
102 × 305 cm
Musée canadien de la photographie contemporaine, Ottawa
2005.91

*Pulvériser, Norman Whaley applique un aphicide* 2004 (planche 4)
De la série *Jardins*
Épreuve à développement chromogène
102 × 122 cm
Avec l'aimable autorisation de l'artiste et de l'Union Gallery, Londres, R.-U.

*Discuter, Michael O'Brian avec artiste et modèle sur sa propriété* 2005 (planche 8)
De la série *Jardins*
Épreuve à développement chromogène
102 × 122 cm
RBC Banque Royale

*Verger de la propriété du D$^{r}$ Young, 3226, 51$^{e}$ rue O., Vancouver* 2005 (planche 10)
De la série *Jardins*
Épreuve au jet d'encre
102 × 305 cm
Collection William J. Hokin

*Reverse Horse, Victoria Moes Practices with Oscar / Reshoeing, Ferrier James Findel with Assistant on Southlands* 2008 (figure 6, plate 12)
From the series *Gardens*
Two ink jet prints in a double-sided frame on plinth
65 × 82 cm
Private Collection, Toronto

*Huntington Botanical Garden, San Marino, California. Desert Garden Nursery with Succulent Collections Donated by Virginia Martin and Seymour Lyndon, Spring* 2005 (plate 13)
From the series *Empire*
Ink jet print
102 × 409 cm
Collection of William and Ruth True, Seattle

*Agave americana variegata* 2006 (plate 17)
From the series *Empire*
Ink jet print
62 × 70 cm
Collection of Enrico Pallotta and Brigitte Laforest

*Aloe principis* 2006 (plate 14)
From the series *Empire*
Ink jet print
64 × 71 cm
Courtesy of the Artist

*Echinocactus grusonii* 2006 (plate 16)
From the series *Empire*
Ink jet print
62 × 70 cm
Private Collection, Toronto

*Euphorbia ingens* 2006 (plate 15)
From the series *Empire*
Ink jet print
71 × 64 cm
Courtesy of the Artist

*Opuntia pittieri* 2006 (plate 18)
From the series *Empire*
Ink jet print
70 × 62 cm
From the collection of David Allison and Chris Nicholson, Vancouver

*Washingtonia filifera* 2006 (plate 19)
From the series *Empire*
Ink jet print
64 × 71 cm
Courtesy of the Artist and Monte Clark Gallery, Vancouver

*Display for Porcupines (Hystrix africae australis), Zoologischer Garten, Berlin* 2006 (plate 32)
Ink jet print
102 × 333 cm
Collection of Mike MacBain

*Hampstead Reservoir Observatory at Lower Terrace, near Whitestone Pond* (edition 2/5) 2006 (not illustrated)
From the series *Hampstead*
Ink jet print
77.5 × 117 cm
Collection of Steve F. Roth

*Hampstead Reservoir Observatory at Lower Terrace, near Whitestone Pond* (edition 3/5) 2006 (plate 23)
From the series *Hampstead*
Ink jet print
77.5 × 117 cm
Courtesy Byron Aceman, Vancouver

*View of Rooke House, Looking Towards Highgate* (edition 1/5) 2006 (plate 26)
From the series *Hampstead*
Ink jet print
76 × 91 cm
Collection of Steve F. Roth

*Hill Garden Pergola at Inverforth House* (edition 2/5) 2007 (plate 29)
From the series *Hampstead*
Ink jet print
66 × 81 cm
Collection of Karen and Richard Pilosof, Toronto

*Hill Garden Pergola at Inverforth House* (edition 3/5) 2007 (plate 25)
From the series *Hampstead*
Ink jet print
66 × 81 cm
Private Collection, Toronto

*View of Vale of Health, Looking Towards Hampstead* (edition 1/5) 2007 (plate 20)
From the series *Hampstead*
Ink jet print
74 × 108 cm
Collection of Susan and Michael Rich

*View of Vale of Health, Looking Towards Hampstead* (edition 5/5) 2007 (plate 28)
From the series *Hampstead*
Ink jet print
74 × 108 cm
Collection of Michael Nininger

*Écuries de la propriété du D$^{r}$ Young, 3226, 51$^{e}$ rue O., Vancouver* 2005 (planche 11)
De la série *Jardins*
Épreuve au jet d'encre
102 × 305 cm
Collection William J. Hokin

*Cheval en marche arrière, Victoria Moes s'entraîne avec Oscar / Nouveau ferrage, le maréchal-ferrant James Findel avec son adjoint dans les Southlands* 2008
(figure 6, planche 12)
De la série *Jardins*
Deux épreuves au jet d'encre dans un cadre double face sur socle
65 × 82 cm
Collection particulière, Toronto

*Huntington Botanical Garden, San Marino, Californie. Pépinière du jardin désertique avec les collections de plantes grasses données par Virginia Martin et Seymour Lyndon, printemps* 2005 (planche 13)
De la série *Empire*
Épreuve au jet d'encre
102 × 409 cm
Collection de William et Ruth True, Seattle

*Agave americana variegata* 2006 (planche 17)
De la série *Empire*
Épreuve au jet d'encre
62 × 70 cm
Collection d'Enrico Pallotta et Brigitte Laforest

*Aloe principis* 2006 (planche 14)
De la série *Empire*
Épreuve au jet d'encre
64 × 71 cm
Avec l'aimable autorisation de l'artiste

*Echinocactus grusonii* 2006 (planche 16)
De la série *Empire*
Épreuve au jet d'encre
62 × 70 cm
Collection particulière, Toronto

*Euphorbia ingens* 2006 (planche 15)
De la série *Empire*
Épreuve au jet d'encre
71 × 64 cm
Avec l'aimable autorisation de l'artiste

*Opuntia pittieri* 2006 (planche 18)
De la série *Empire*
Épreuve au jet d'encre
70 × 62 cm
De la collection de David Allison et Chris Nicholson, Vancouver

*Washingtonia filifera* 2006 (planche 19)
De la série *Empire*
Épreuve au jet d'encre
64 × 71 cm
Avec l'aimable autorisation de l'artiste et de la Monte Clark Gallery, Vancouver

*Enclos des porcs-épics (Hystrix africae australis), Zoologischer Garten, Berlin* 2006
(planche 32)
Épreuve au jet d'encre
102 × 333 cm
Collection de Mike MacBain

*Hampstead Observatory au sommet du réservoir à Lower Terrace, près de Whitestone Pond* (édition 2/5) 2006
(non reproduite)
De la série *Hampstead*
Épreuve au jet d'encre
77,5 × 117 cm
Collection de Steve F. Roth

*Hampstead Observatory au sommet du réservoir à Lower Terrace, près de Whitestone Pond* (édition 3/5) 2006
(planche 23)
De la série *Hampstead*
Épreuve au jet d'encre
77,5 × 117 cm
Avec l'aimable autorisation de Byron Aceman, Vancouver

*Vue de Rooke House, vers Highgate* (édition 1/5) 2006
(planche 26)
De la série *Hampstead*
Épreuve au jet d'encre
76 × 91 cm
Collection de Steve F. Roth

*Pergola de Hill Garden, Inverforth House* (édition 2/5)
2007 (planche 29)
De la série *Hampstead*
Épreuve au jet d'encre
66 × 81 cm
Collection de Karen et Richard Pilosof, Toronto

*Fallen Oak Tree* (edition 2/5) 2008 (plate 22)
From the series *Hampstead*
Ink jet print
68.5 × 61 cm
Courtesy Byron Aceman, Vancouver

*Gorse and Sky* (edition 2/5) 2008 (plate 21)
From the series *Hampstead*
Ink jet print
51 × 60 cm
Collection of Steven Casey, Toronto

*Gorse and Sky* (edition 4/5) 2008 (plate 30)
From the series *Hampstead*
Ink jet print
51 × 60 cm
Collection of Daniel Faria, Toronto

*Judges Walk, Looking Towards Jack Straw Castle*
(edition 1/5) 2008 (plate 27)
From the series *Hampstead*
Ink jet print
51 × 191 cm
Courtesy Matt Hammatt, Bellingham, WA



*Trees and Sky, West Heath* (edition 2/5) 2008 (plate 24)
From the series *Hampstead*
Ink jet print
56 × 69 cm
Courtesy of the Artist and Monte Clark Gallery, Toronto

*Emptied Penguin Pool, London Zoo, May 2008,*
*Architect: Berthold Lubetkin, 1934* 2008 (plate 31)
Ink jet print
76 × 267 cm
Courtesy of the Artist

*A Horse Drawn Hearse, Queens Royal Tours, 174 Anne,*
*Niagara-on-the-Lake, Ontario* 2009 (plate 33)
Ink jet print
152 × 305 cm
Courtesy of the Artist

*Pergola de Hill Garden, Inverforth House* (édition 3/5) 2007 (planche 25)
De la série *Hampstead*
Épreuve au jet d'encre
66 × 81 cm
Collection particulière, Toronto

*Vue de Vale of Health, vers Hampstead* (édition 1/5) 2007 (planche 20)
De la série *Hampstead*
Épreuve au jet d'encre
74 × 108 cm
Collection de Susan et Michael Rich

*Vue de Vale of Health, vers Hampstead* (édition 5/5) 2007 (planche 28)
De la série *Hampstead*
Épreuve au jet d'encre
74 × 108 cm
Collection de Michael Nininger

*Chêne mort* (édition 2/5) 2008 (planche 22)
De la série *Hampstead*
Épreuve au jet d'encre
68,5 × 61 cm
Avec l'aimable autorisation de Byron Aceman, Vancouver

*Ajonc et ciel* (édition 2/5) 2008 (planche 21)
De la série *Hampstead*
Épreuve au jet d'encre
51 × 60 cm
Collection de Steven Casey, Toronto

*Ajonc et ciel* (édition 4/5) 2008 (planche 30)
De la série *Hampstead*
Épreuve au jet d'encre
51 × 60 cm
Collection de Daniel Faria, Toronto

*Judges Walk, vers Jack Straw Castle* (édition 1/5) 2008 (planche 27)
De la série *Hampstead*
Épreuve au jet d'encre
51 × 191 cm
Avec l'aimable autorisation de Matt Hammatt, Bellingham, WA

*Arbres et ciel, West Heath* (édition 2/5) 2008 (planche 24)
De la série *Hampstead*
Épreuve au jet d'encre
56 × 69 cm
Avec l'aimable autorisation de l'artiste et de la Monte Clark Gallery, Toronto

*Piscine de manchots vide, London Zoo, mai 2008, architecte : Berthold Lubetkin, 1934* 2008 (planche 31)
Épreuve au jet d'encre
76 × 267 cm
Avec l'aimable autorisation de l'artiste

*Un corbillard hippomobile, Queens Royal Tours, 174, Anne, Niagara-on-the-Lake, Ontario* 2009 (planche 33)
Épreuve au jet d'encre
152 × 305 cm
Avec l'aimable autorisation de l'artiste

**Photo credits**
All photographs by Scott McFarland have been provided courtesy of the artist, Monte Clark Gallery (Vancouver and Toronto) and Regen Projects (Los Angeles)
Fig. 3, 5 and 7: National Gallery of Canada
Fig. 4: Photo © NGC

**Library and Archives Canada Cataloguing in Publication**
Kunard, Andrea.
Scott McFarland: a cultivated view = la réalité aménagée.
Exhibition catalogue.
Text in English and French.
ISBN 978-0-88884-861-1

1. McFarland, Scott, 1975– Exhibitions. 2. Photography, Artistic – Exhibitions. I. McFarland, Scott, 1975–. II. Canadian Museum of Contemporary Photography. III. Title. IV. Title: Cultivated view. V. Title: Réalité aménagée.

TR647 M315 2009 779'.092 C2009-986000-7E

**Crédits photographiques**
Toutes les photographies de Scott McFarland sont reproduites avec l'aimable autorisation de l'artiste, de la Monte Clark Gallery (Vancouver et Toronto) et de la galerie Regen Projects (Los Angeles).
Fig. 3, 5 et 7 : Musée des beaux-arts du Canada
Fig. 4 : photo © MBAC

**Catalogage avant publication de Bibliothèque et Archives Canada**
Kunard, Andrea.
Scott McFarland : a cultivated view = la réalité aménagée.
Catalogue d'exposition.
Texte en anglais et en français.
ISBN 978-0-88884-861-1

1. McFarland, Scott, 1975– –Expositions. 2. Photographie, artistique–Expositions. I. McFarland, Scott, 1975–. II. Musée canadien de la photographie contemporaine. III. Titre. IV. Titre : Cultivated view. V. Titre : Réalité aménagée.

TR647 M315 2009 779'.092 C2009-986000-7F